Power of a Woman Series

The
Bottom Line

Dr. Cassundra White-Elliott

This book is a work of non-fiction. All scripture are from the New International Version of the Holy Bible, except where otherwise noted.

CLF Publishing, LLC.
9161 Sierra Ave, Ste. 203C
Fontana, CA 92335
www.clfpublishing.org

Copyright © 2015 by Cassundra White-Elliott. All rights reserved. No portion of this book may be reproduced, stored in a retrieval system, or transmitted by any form or any means electronically, photocopied, recorded, or any other except for brief quotations in printed reviews, without the prior permission of the publisher.

Cover Design by Senir Design. Contact information- info@senirdesign.com.

ISBN # 978-0-9961971-1-3

Printed in the United States of America.

Dedications

This book is dedicated to anyone who has ever had a trial and has struggled to understand 'why.'

Acknowledgments

*I acknowledge the Father, the Son, and the Holy Spirit
for walking me step by step through
the writing of the book.*

*I, literally, could not have done it
without the three of you.*

Table of Contents

Introduction	9
Chapter One	13
The Foundation: And So It Begins	
Chapter Two	21
The Sabotage Continues…	
Chapter Three	27
A Painful Utterance	
Chapter Four	31
Completely Misunderstood	
Chapter Five	35
Let Me Repeat Myself	
Chapter Six	41
Then Comes Another	
Chapter Seven	45
Allow Me to Respond	
Chapter Eight	49
Flowing Like a River	
Chapter Nine	53
No Punches Withheld	
Chapter Ten	57
Knowledge Reigns Supreme	

Chapter Eleven	65
Fiery Darts	
Chapter Twelve	69
Woe Is Me!	
Chapter Thirteen	73
The Verbal Attacks Continue	
Chapter Fourteen	77
Cease and Desist	
Chapter Fifteen	83
The Wicked vs The Blessed	
Chapter Sixteen	87
God is Just	
Chapter Seventeen	91
Putting Others First	
Chapter Eighteen	95
Suffering for the Righteous	
Chapter Nineteen	99
God's Sovereignty	
Chapter Twenty	101
Declaration of Innocence	
Chapter Twenty-One	105
Curiosity	
Chapter Twenty-Two	107
One Final Thought	

Chapter Twenty-Three	115
An Interjection	
Chapter Twenty-Four	127
A Voice of Thunder	
Chapter Twenty-Five	135
A Heartfelt Apology	
Chapter Twenty-Six	137
Abundant Blessings	
Chapter Twenty-Seven	141
Final Thoughts	
References	145
Gift of Salvation	147
Other Books by the Author	155

Dr. C. White-Elliott

Introduction

Why an Exegesis?

A few months ago, the Book of Job was the topic of several lessons I taught (for Sunday school and other Bible classes) and also different sermons I was blessed to hear (one from my pastor on one particular Sunday, as well as two different pastors on the radio during the same week). When the topic continued to surface in the short time frame of two to three weeks, I knew it was more than purely coincidental. I knew Holy Spirit was speaking to me. However, it wasn't until after I reached the last lesson on the Book of Job in my Adult Sunday School class and I began to articulate to my students the overall meaning of the Book of Job that I understood the purpose of the reoccurring discussions.

There are many lessons to be learned from Job's catastrophic experience. However, when the story ended by God drawing a conclusion to the whole matter, I found there is an overall bottom line to Job's experience. There is one comprehensive message as a culminating sum of all the messages embedded within. As you read this detailed chapter-by-chapter exegesis of the Book of Job, the comprehensive message Holy Spirit revealed to me will begin to unfold for you.

Like Job, each experience we encounter is designed to teach us a lesson. There is a bottom line. However, it is up to us for how long it takes to learn the lesson and whether we accept it or not.

To assist in your understanding of the Book of Job, the messages within, and the bottom line of the complete text, an exegesis will be performed.

What is an exegesis?

Exegesis (/ˌɛksəˈdʒiːsəs/; from the Greek ἐξήγησις from ἐξηγεῖσθαι 'to lead out') is a critical explanation or interpretation of a text, particularly a religious text. Traditionally, the term was used primarily for exegesis of the Bible; however, in modern usage "biblical exegesis" is used for greater specificity to distinguish it from any other broader critical text explanation.

Exegesis includes a wide range of critical disciplines: textual criticism is the investigation into the history and origins of the text, but exegesis may include the study of the historical and cultural backgrounds for the author, the text, and the original audience. Other analysis includes classification of the type of literary genres present in the text, and an analysis of grammatical and syntactical features in the text itself. Further, the terms 'exegesis' and 'hermeneutics' have been used interchangeably.

Scope of the Exegesis

The exegesis I will present will be an extrapolation of the text, an explanation of what the text means, and the messages God is communicating to us. This will be done while providing surrounding context about the key participants in the Book of

Job and the circumstances in which the story is set and takes place.

Layout of the chapters

Each chapter of this book will include a chapter or several consecutive chapters from the Book of Job along with an explanation of surrounding context and a detailed interpretation, until all forty-two chapters of the Book of Job have been examined and discussed.

The Bottom Line

Chapter One

The Foundation: And So It Begins

Book of Job Chapter 1- Prologue

In the land of Uz there lived a man whose name was Job. This man was blameless and upright; he feared God and shunned evil. ² He had seven sons and three daughters, ³ and he owned seven thousand sheep, three thousand camels, five hundred yoke of oxen and five hundred donkeys, and had a large number of servants. He was the greatest man among all the people of the East. ⁴ His sons used to hold feasts in their homes on their birthdays, and they would invite their three sisters to eat and drink with them. ⁵ When a period of feasting had run its course, Job would make arrangements for them to be purified. Early in the morning he would sacrifice a burnt offering for each of them, thinking, "Perhaps my children have sinned and cursed God in their hearts." This was Job's regular custom. ⁶ One day the angels came to present themselves before the L<small>ORD</small>, and Satan also came with them. ⁷ The L<small>ORD</small> said to Satan, "Where have you come from?" Satan answered the L<small>ORD</small>, "From roaming throughout the earth, going back and forth on it." ⁸ Then the L<small>ORD</small> said to Satan, "Have you considered my servant Job? There is no one on earth like him; he is blameless and upright, a man who fears God and shuns evil." ⁹ "Does Job fear God for nothing?"

*Satan replied. ¹⁰ "Have you not put a hedge around him and his household and everything he has? You have blessed the work of his hands, so that his flocks and herds are spread throughout the land. ¹¹ But now stretch out your hand and strike everything he has, and he will surely curse you to your face." ¹² The L*ORD *said to Satan, "Very well, then, everything he has is in your power, but on the man himself do not lay a finger." Then Satan went out from the presence of the L*ORD*. ¹³ One day when Job's sons and daughters were feasting and drinking wine at the oldest brother's house, ¹⁴ a messenger came to Job and said, "The oxen were plowing and the donkeys were grazing nearby, ¹⁵ and the Sabeans attacked and made off with them. They put the servants to the sword, and I am the only one who has escaped to tell you!" ¹⁶ While he was still speaking, another messenger came and said, "The fire of God fell from the heavens and burned up the sheep and the servants, and I am the only one who has escaped to tell you!" ¹⁷ While he was still speaking, another messenger came and said, "The Chaldeans formed three raiding parties and swept down on your camels and made off with them. They put the servants to the sword, and I am the only one who has escaped to tell you!" ¹⁸ While he was still speaking, yet another messenger came and said, "Your sons and daughters were feasting and drinking wine at the oldest brother's house, ¹⁹ when suddenly a mighty wind swept in from the desert and struck the four corners of the house. It collapsed on them and they are dead, and I am the only one who has escaped to tell you!" ²⁰ At this, Job got up and tore his robe and shaved his head. Then he fell to the ground in worship ²¹ and said: "Naked I came from my mother's womb, and* *naked I will depart. The LORD gave and the LORD has taken away; may the name of the LORD be praised." ²² In all this, Job did not sin by charging God with wrongdoing.*

At the beginning of Chapter 1, we are introduced to the primary character of this book- Job. He is said to have resided in the land of Uz. "Uz is sometimes identified with the kingdom of Edom, roughly in the area of modern-day southwestern Jordan and southern Israel. Lamentations 4:21 reads: 'Rejoice and be glad, O daughter of Edom, that dwellest in the land of Uz.' According to the Dead Sea document, The War Scroll, the land of Uz is mentioned as existing somewhere beyond the Euphrates possibly in relation to Aram, a direct descendant of Shem (Genesis 10:23)" (Bury, 1911).

Job is described as 'blameless and upright.' Does that mean he was without sin? Of course not. Romans 3:23 clearly states without doubt or compromise, *"for all have sinned and fall short of the glory of God."* Only one exception to this statement is given in the Bible. That exception speaks of the Lord Jesus Christ. *"God made him who had no sin to be sin for us, so that in him we might become the righteousness of God"* (II Corinthians 5:21). Therefore, Jesus is the only one who lived on Earth who was sinless.

So then, what does the statement 'blameless and upright' mean? 'Blameless' refers to a person of integrity as it relates to his relationship with God. In Job's relationship with the Lord, he operated in the spirit of integrity. The use of the word 'upright,' means Job walked uprightly before the Lord. When we walk uprightly before the Lord, God's righteousness is imputed upon us. We, therefore, walk in the righteousness of

Christ. Does it mean we are without sin? No, it means our sins our forgiven, and we do not carry the blame of them.

Further, Job is described as being wealthy- both in family and riches. He was the richest man in the east, as demonstrated by the number of cattle and sheep he was said to have, along with seven sons and three daughters. More importantly, Job was a man who wanted to honor God at all times and was concerned about the spiritual condition of his children. He was a pious man (devoutly religious). So, after his children's times of celebrations (which most likely involved wild partying and drunkenness), Job always offered a sacrifice on their behalf. The purpose of the sacrifice was cleansing from sin and God's glorification. Job wanted to be sure any sin committed covertly (not openly displayed) or overtly (done or shown openly/plainly apparent) (Oxford Dictionary) were blotted out.

One day, the heavenly hosts (the angels) came into the presence of the Lord, and accompanying them came the angel of darkness, Satan. Upon seeing Satan, our adversary, God questioned him asking from where he had come. Satan responded to God by telling him he had come from roaming the earth. God immediately responded, "Have you considered my servant Job?" Why did He respond that way? The book of I Peter says, *"Be sober, be vigilant; because your adversary the devil, as a roaring lion, walketh about, seeking whom he may devour"* (5:8, KJV). So, Satan's actions told God what his agenda was: He was seeking someone to chastise, or he was seeking someone who was disobedient to God, a believer who had sinned, for the very purpose of exposing the sin to God. Revelation 12:10 states, *"And I heard a loud voice saying in heaven, Now is come salvation, and strength, and the kingdom of our God, and the power of his Christ: for the accuser of our brethren is cast down, which accused them before our God day and night"* (KJV). Satan constantly goes before God and rats on the believers, telling God of their evil doings. This is interesting because God is omniscient; He knows everything. He doesn't need a spy to report to Him.

After Satan's statement, God took Satan's roaming, in this particular instance, as an opportunity to teach a lesson. To whom was the lesson being taught? You will shortly find out.

At that moment, God's plan went into action with the following suggestion: "Have you considered my servant Job?" Satan had obviously considered Job because he knew there was a hedge of protection around Job. He knew because Job was a servant of God, he was untouchable. In order to inflict any harm upon Job, in any form, Satan would need the express permission of the one who holds complete control: God.

Also worth noting is God's description of Job: my servant. God's reference to a human in this manner demonstrates "the highest compliment the Old Testament ever pays to human beings. The concept of servant combined overtones of obedience, worship, and faithfulness" (Hahn, 2012).

After Satan questioned God about the hedge He had placed around Job as a protective force, he continued talking, making his first accusation. Satan stated, *"But now stretch out your hand and strike everything he has, and he will surely curse you to your face"* (v. 11). Satan was forcefully stating Job was only honoring God because God had blessed him and favored him. Satan believed if God removed all He had blessed Job with, Job would most certainly curse God. With his insolent statement,

Satan had taken the bait! God responded by giving Satan permission to attack Job, *with one restriction-* Satan could **not** lay a finger on Job himself. That meant Satan could not cause any physical harm to Job: only his possessions and his family.

Having obtained God's permission to have his way with Job, Satan departed from God's presence and wasted no time wreaking havoc in Job's life. The next scene in Chapter One occurs on Earth with Job and his family. It appears to be business as usual because Job's children are said to be *"feasting and drinking wine at the older brother's house"* (v. 13). Meanwhile, Job received a succession of devastating and mind-boggling news:

> A series of four messengers [went] running to Job with a succession of bad news. It is interesting that the order in which Job's losses are reported is opposite the order in which his blessings were enumerated. The result is that the climax of tragedy is the death of Job's children. The blessings of children, flocks and camels, and herds and donkeys proceeded from the most important to the least. By beginning with the loss of the herds and donkeys and moving to flocks and camels, the author builds up the tense expectation of the worst possible news regarding Job's children. (Hahn, 2012)

Not many of us would have had the same response Job had after receiving bad news four times in a row, with each report worse than the previous. After the last messenger delivered his message, Job tore his robe, shaved his head and fell down to worship God while "acknowledg[ing] that he had entered life with nothing and that he would take nothing with him. He affirmed that the God who had given him all these blessings had the right to withdraw them at any time" (Hahn, 2012). Our response may have started the way Job's did with him tearing his robe. We may have torn something also or even broken something. But notice this, Job's action was symbolic of experiencing grief.

In the Ancient Near East, one of the primary ways people expressed their grief was by tearing their clothes. This practice is common in the Bible and can be confusing at times to those who don't understand the symbolism behind the action. Reuben is the first person recorded in the Bible as tearing his clothes. He was the oldest son of Jacob, and one of the 11 brothers who betrayed Joseph and sold him as a slave to traders bound for Egypt. Reuben wanted to save Joseph, but was unwilling to stand up to his other siblings. Reuben planned to rescue Joseph in secret from the cistern (or pit) the brothers had thrown him into. But after finding out that Joseph had been sold as a slave, he reacted in a passionate display of emotion: *"When Reuben returned to the cistern and saw that Joseph was not there, he tore his clothes. 30 He went back to his brothers and said, "The boy isn't there! Where can I turn now?"* (Genesis 37:29-30). (O'Neal, 2014)

Our response, on the other hand, may have been altogether for a different reason. Usually tearing or breaking something in our modern society is an outward demonstration of anger. With this we must be careful, for the Bible says, *"'Be angry, and do not sin': do not let the sun go down on your wrath"*

(Ephesians 4:26). From this verse, we understand anger is a human emotion, but we should not allow it to cause us to sin.

The statement Job uttered ended with, *"may the name of the Lord be praised"* (v. 21b). Even in the midst of calamity, Job found it within his heart to praise God. This demonstrates Job's level of commitment to God, as well as his level of honor and respect for God. Many times, we find it difficult to praise God in the midst of adversity because we have difficulty conceptualizing certain events. God is acutely aware of our lacking mental aptitude for discerning spiritual matters; thus, He tells us in Isaiah 55:8, *"For my thoughts are not your thoughts, neither are your ways my ways," declares the LORD."* Job did not try to reason with God. He accepted the reality of the situation even while understanding escaped him.

Chapter Two

The Sabotage Continues…

Book of Job Chapter 2

On another day the angels came to present themselves before the Lord, and Satan also came with them to present himself before him. ² And the Lord said to Satan, "Where have you come from?" Satan answered the Lord, "From roaming throughout the earth, going back and forth on it." ³ Then the Lord said to Satan, "Have you considered my servant Job? There is no one on earth like him; he is blameless and upright, a man who fears God and shuns evil. And he still maintains his integrity, though you incited me against him to ruin him without any reason." ⁴ "Skin for skin!" Satan replied. "A man will give all he has for his own life. ⁵ But now stretch out your hand and strike his flesh and bones, and he will surely curse you to your face." ⁶ The Lord said to Satan, "Very well, then, he is in your hands; but you must spare his life." ⁷ So Satan went out from the presence of the Lord and afflicted Job with painful sores from the soles of his feet to the crown of his head. ⁸ Then Job took a piece of broken pottery and scraped himself with it as he sat among the ashes. ⁹ His wife said to him, "Are you still maintaining your integrity? Curse God and die!" ¹⁰ He replied, "You are talking like a foolish woman. Shall we accept good from God, and not trouble?" In all this, Job did not sin in what he said. ⁱⁱ When Job's three friends, Eliphaz the Temanite, Bildad the Shuhite and Zophar the Naamathite, heard about all the troubles that had come upon him, they set out from their homes and met together by agreement to go and sympathize with him and comfort him. ¹² When they saw him from a distance, they could hardly recognize him; they began to weep aloud, and they tore their robes and sprinkled dust on their heads. ¹³ Then they sat on the ground with him for seven days and seven nights. No one said a word to him, because they saw how great his suffering was.

The first three and a half verses of Chapter 2 mirror verses 6-8 in Chapter 1. Thus, the second conversation God had with Satan (regarding Job) began in the same manner as the first conversation they had, but the conversation eventually took a different turn but concluded with nearly the same result. In the latter portion of verse three, God declared, *"And he still maintains his integrity, though you incited me against him to ruin him without any reason"* (v. 3b). Then, Satan replied with a challenge: *"Skin for skin!" Satan replied. "A man will give all he has for his own life. But now stretch out your hand and strike his flesh and bones, and he will surely curse you to your face"* (v. 4). After this accusatory statement, God's response was similar to what it was before when Satan made his first accusation against Job. God again gave Satan permission to do as he pleased with Job. But once again, there was an exception: Satan could **not** take Job's life.

After having been granted permission to inflict physical pain upon Job's person, Satan went and did just that. He covered Job's body with painful sores from the crown of his head to the soles of his feet. But Job held fast to his integrity. He did not curse God. Instead, he sat in a pile of ashes and scraped himself with a piece of broken pottery.

The devil tempts his own children, and draws them to sin, and afterwards torments, when he has brought them to ruin; but this child of God [Job], he tormented with affliction, and then tempted to make a bad use of his affliction. He provoked Job to curse God. The disease was very grievous. If at any time we are tried with sore and grievous distempers, let us not think ourselves dealt with otherwise than as God sometimes deals with the best of his saints and servants. Job humbled himself under the mighty hand of God, and brought his mind to his condition. His wife was spared to him, to be a troubler and tempter to him. Satan still endeavours to draw men from God, as he did our first parents, by suggesting hard thoughts of Him, than which nothing is more false. But Job resisted and overcame the temptation. Shall we, guilty, polluted, worthless creatures, receive so many unmerited blessings from a just and holy God, and shall we refuse to accept the punishment of our sins, when we suffer so much less than we deserve? Let murmuring, as well as boasting, be forever done away. Thus far Job stood the trial, and appeared brightest in the furnace of affliction. There might be risings of corruption in his heart, but grace had the upper hand (Henry, 2014).

As stated in the excerpt from Matthew Henry's Commentary above, of all the losses Job suffered, he did not suffer the loss of his wife. The life of his wife was spared. I suspect Satan new her heart and her temperament. He knew he could use her as a pawn to tempt her husband to curse God and to turn his back on Him. In verse nine, she did just that when she stated, *"Are you still maintaining your integrity? Curse God and die!"* (v. 9). From his wife's insidious question and command, Job became indignant. He replied, *"You are talking like a foolish woman. Shall we accept good from God, and not trouble?"* (v. 10).

Job raised an excellent point! We believers often times only want to experience the blessings of God. We have a difficult time with hardship and calamity and even acknowledging God is capable of permitting them to happen to us. But whether we want to accept it or not, that is reality.

After Job's brief discussion with his wife, he yet failed to sin.

Just like today, word of bad news traveled fast back then. Having heard the news of Job's misfortune, Job's three friends arrived on the scene together with the intent to sympathize with him and bring him comfort. One friend was Eliphaz, the Temanite. "The word Temanite probably indicates that he was an Edomite, or member of a Palestinian people descended from Esau" (The Encyclopædia Britannica, 2014). The second friend was Bildad, the Shuhite, "probably a member of a nomadic tribe dwelling in southeastern Palestine" (The Encyclopædia Britannica, 2014). The third friend was Zophar, the Naamathite, "one who dwells in Naamah, perhaps a region in Arabia" (The Encyclopædia Britannica, 2014).

When the three friends reached Job and witnessed his condition for themselves, their response demonstrated their love for their friend. Just as Job had poured ashes on his head and tore his clothing when he learned of the calamity (including the loss of his children), his three friends immediately tore their robes and sprinkled dust upon their heads as they wept loudly. They too were in deep anguish, along with Job, as they felt his pain. Then, without speaking a word, they sat on the ground with him for seven days and seven nights. "That they would sit in silence for seven days also signifies how deeply they share Job's sorrow" (Hahn, 2012).

So they sat down with him upon the ground seven days and seven nights, which was the usual time of mourning, (Genesis 50:10); not that they were in this posture all this time, without sleeping, eating, or drinking, and other necessaries of life; but they came and sat with him every day and night for seven days and nights running, and sat the far greater part of them with him, conforming themselves to him and sympathizing with him: and none spake a word unto him; concerning his affliction and the cause of it, and what they thought about it; partly through the loss they were at concerning it, hesitating in their minds, and having some suspicion of evil in Job; and partly through the grief of their own hearts, and the vehemence of their passions, but chiefly because of the case and circumstances Job was in, as follows: for they saw that his grief was very great; and they knew not well what comfort to administer, and were fearful lest they should add grief to grief; or they saw that his "grief increased exceedingly" (r); his boils, during these seven days, grew sorer and sorer, and his pain became more intolerable, that there was no speaking to him until he was a little at ease (Gill, 2004-2014).

The Bottom Line

Chapter Three
A Painful Utterance

Book of Job Chapter 3 Job Speaks

After this, Job opened his mouth and cursed the day of his birth. ² He said: ³ "May the day of my birth perish, and the night that said, 'A boy is conceived!' ⁴ That day—may it turn to darkness; may God above not care about it; may no light shine on it. ⁵ May gloom and utter darkness claim it once more; may a cloud settle over it; may blackness overwhelm it. ⁶ That night—may thick darkness seize it; may it not be included among the days of the year nor be entered in any of the months. ⁷ May that night be barren; may no shout of joy be heard in it. ⁸ May those who curse days curse that day, those who are ready to rouse Leviathan. ⁹ May its morning stars become dark; may it wait for daylight in vain and not see the first rays of dawn, ¹⁰ for it did not shut the doors of the womb on me to hide trouble from my eyes. ¹¹ "Why did I not perish at birth, and die as I came from the womb? ¹² Why were there knees to receive me and breasts that I might be nursed? ¹³ For now I would be lying down in peace; I would be asleep and at rest ¹⁴ with kings and rulers of the earth, who built for themselves places now lying in ruins ¹⁵ with princes who had gold, who filled their houses with silver. ¹⁶ Or why was I not hidden away in the ground like a stillborn child, like an infant *who never saw the light of day? ^{17} There the wicked cease from turmoil, and there the weary are at rest. ^{18} Captives also enjoy their ease; they no longer hear the slave driver's shout. ^{19} The small and the great are there, and the slaves are freed from their owners. ^{20} "Why is light given to those in misery, and life to the bitter of soul, ^{21} to those who long for death that does not come, who search for it more than for hidden treasure, ^{22} who are filled with gladness and rejoice when they reach the grave? ^{23} Why is life given to a man whose way is hidden, whom God has hedged in? ^{24} For sighing has become my daily food; my groans pour out like water. ^{25} What I feared has come upon me; what I dreaded has happened to me. ^{26} I have no peace, no quietness; I have no rest, but only turmoil."*

After the seven days of silence for Job and his friends, Job broke the silence by proclaiming a curse on the day he was born. From verse one to verse ten, Job shared his desire of that day to have never existed and to be remembered by no one. He questioned why darkness could not have surrounded it and why it could not have been barren- not giving life to him. He then asked for it to be removed from the calendar all together.

In verses eleven through nineteen, Job spoke at great length about death. He questioned why he could not have died at birth. Then, he went on to state how those who have experienced death are at rest, whether their existence was 'wicked' or 'weary.'

From versus twenty to twenty-six, Job questioned the earthly conditions of those who suffer continuously, as he wondered why 'the light' could not be removed from them. The chapter closes with Job stating he has no rest, but instead, he is filled with turmoil.

Job knew full well time could not be reversed and the details surrounding his birth changed. What then did he hope to gain from such an in-depth and lengthy monologue? Job was very desperately expressing his deep anguish and was lamenting. He could not reverse his birth, but he could request an end to his suffering. So, he was begging for his life to come to an end. He didn't believe it was fair for one who did not desire to be alive to be forced to do so.

Plainly and simply, Job was suffering deep emotional and physical pain, and he wanted it to end—quickly. So, he made his desires known.

Philippians 4:6 says, *"Do not be anxious about anything, but in every situation, by prayer and petition, with thanksgiving, present your requests to God."* Therefore, all our hopes and desires are to be presented to the throne of God. And we should wait patiently for God to respond. Giving Him a deadline to respond is not waiting patiently. We must remember God's time is not our time. We operate in the realm of time; while, God operates in eternity.

Another point- presenting our desires to God and having them granted do not necessarily coincide. Just because we desire something does not mean our desires will be honored by God. Having God stamp our request 'denied' should not be viewed negatively because God knows what is best for us, and we would be wise to trust His judgment.

To prevent disappointment and heartache regarding our requests, we should always seek the Father's desires for our lives. We should pray that His will is done in our lives. When we adopt this mindset, we are exercising our faith in God and releasing our will and accepting His will for us.

Wouldn't you be more satisfied and fulfilled with the choices God makes for you than your own?

Chapter Four

Completely Misunderstood

Book of Job Chapter 4 Eliphaz

Then Eliphaz the Temanite replied: ^{2} "If someone ventures a word with you, will you be impatient? But who can keep from speaking? ^{3} Think how you have instructed many, how you have strengthened feeble hands. ^{4} Your words have supported those who stumbled; you have strengthened faltering knees. ^{5} But now trouble comes to you, and you are discouraged; it strikes you, and you are dismayed. ^{6} Should not your piety be your confidence and your blameless ways your hope? ^{7} "Consider now: Who, being innocent, has ever perished? Where were the upright ever destroyed? ^{8} As I have observed, those who plow evil and those who sow trouble reap it. ^{9} At the breath of God they perish; at the blast of his anger they are no more. ^{10} The lions may roar and growl, yet the teeth of the great lions are broken. ^{11} The lion perishes for lack of prey, and the cubs of the lioness are scattered. ^{12} "A word was secretly brought to me, my ears caught a whisper of it. ^{13} Amid disquieting dreams in the night, when deep sleep falls on people, ^{14} fear and trembling seized me and made all my bones shake. ^{15} A spirit glided past my face, and the hair on my body stood on end. ^{16} It stopped, but I could not tell what it was. A form stood before my eyes, and I heard a hushed voice: ^{17} 'Can a mortal be more righteous than God? Can even a strong man be more pure than his Maker? ^{18} If God places no trust in his servants, if he charges his angels with error, ^{19} how much more those who live in houses of clay, whose foundations are in the dust, who are crushed more readily than a moth! ^{20} Between dawn and dusk they are broken to pieces; unnoticed, they perish forever. ^{21} Are not the cords of their tent pulled up, so that they die without wisdom?'

Book of Job Chapter 5 Eliphaz Continues

"Call if you will, but who will answer you? To which of the holy ones will you turn? ^{2} Resentment kills a fool, and envy slays the simple. ^{3} I myself have seen a fool taking root, but suddenly his house was cursed. ^{4} His children are far from safety, crushed in court without a defender. ^{5} The hungry consume his harvest, taking it even from among thorns, and the thirsty pant after his wealth. ^{6} For hardship does not spring from the soil, nor does trouble sprout from the ground. ^{7} Yet man is born to trouble as surely as sparks fly upward. ^{8} "But if I were you, I would appeal to God; I would lay my cause before him. ^{9} He performs wonders that cannot be fathomed, miracles that cannot be counted. ^{10} He provides rain for the earth; he sends water on the countryside. ^{11} The lowly he sets on high, and those who mourn are lifted to safety. ^{12} He thwarts the plans of the crafty, so that their hands achieve no success. ^{13} He catches the wise in their craftiness, and the schemes of the wily are swept away. ^{14} Darkness comes upon them in the daytime; at noon they grope as in the night. ^{15} He saves the needy from the sword in their mouth; he saves them from the clutches of the powerful. ^{16} So the poor have hope, and injustice shuts its mouth. *¹⁷ "Blessed is the one whom God corrects; so do not despise the discipline of the Almighty. ¹⁸ For he wounds, but he also binds up; he injures, but his hands also heal. ¹⁹ From six calamities he will rescue you; in seven no harm will touch you. ²⁰ In famine he will deliver you from death, and in battle from the stroke of the sword. ²¹ You will be protected from the lash of the tongue, and need not fear when destruction comes. ²² You will laugh at destruction and famine, and need not fear the wild animals. ²³ For you will have a covenant with the stones of the field, and the wild animals will be at peace with you. ²⁴ You will know that your tent is secure; you will take stock of your property and find nothing missing. ²⁵ You will know that your children will be many, and your descendants like the grass of the earth. ²⁶ You will come to the grave in full vigor, like sheaves gathered in season. ²⁷ "We have examined this, and it is true. So hear it and apply it to yourself."*

Chapters 4 and 5 of the Book of Job consist of Eliphaz's response to Job's heartfelt outpouring. At the beginning of his monologue, Eliphaz asks Job if he can remain quiet while another speaks. He also reminds Job of the many lives he had spoken into and how he had helped others on countless times. Eliphaz is troubled because the same person who had counseled others is now troubled when his relationship with God should be able to subdue him. The reality of Job's position of despair, accompanied by his own words, led Eliphaz to draw a conclusion.

The words Eliphaz spoke demonstrate he found Job to have walked in disobedience to God's statutes. Several statements make Eliphaz's position clear. Verse seven questions: *"Consider now: Who, being innocent, has ever perished? Where were the upright ever destroyed?"* With these questions, there is no doubt Eliphaz believes Job is to blame for all he has suffered. To substantiate his position, Eliphaz adds, *"As I have observed, those who plow evil and those who sow trouble reap it. At the breath of God they perish; at the blast of his anger they are no more"* (v. 8). Job has without doubt had troubles heaped upon him. Does that mean, however, he was the one to sow trouble initially?

Romans 5:12 says, *"Therefore, just as sin entered the world through one man, and death through sin, and in this way death came to all people, because all sinned— "* Through this verse, we understand sin entered the natural realm through one man, Adam, and we are now subject to evil doings of Satan, the prince and the power of the air. Satan has a measure of power, as we see here, and he inflicts harm upon those he chooses, with and only with God's permission. Therefore, harm inflicted upon us is not evidence we sinned. God could have another reason for allowing calamities and trials to come our way.

Eliphaz, convinced of Job's wrongdoing, suggests Job repent for whatever wrong he has committed, so he can be restored unto God's graces. He shares with Job how merciful and forgiving God is, but Job's repentance is needed for the trouble he has encountered to cease. Eliphaz encourages him to reach out to God, as He is the only one who can forgive his sin and set him free: "[8] *"But if I were you, I would appeal to God; I would lay my cause before him.* [9] *He performs wonders that cannot be fathomed, miracles that cannot be counted"* (Job 5:8-9).

Chapter Five
Let Me Repeat Myself

Chapter 6 Job

Then Job replied: ² "If only my anguish could be weighed and all my misery be placed on the scales! ³ It would surely outweigh the sand of the seas— no wonder my words have been impetuous. ⁴ The arrows of the Almighty are in me, my spirit drinks in their poison; God's terrors are marshaled against me. ⁵ Does a wild donkey bray when it has grass, or an ox bellow when it has fodder? ⁶ Is tasteless food eaten without salt, or is there flavor in the sap of the mallow? ⁷ I refuse to touch it; such food makes me ill. ⁸ "Oh, that I might have my request, that God would grant what I hope for, ⁹ that God would be willing to crush me, to let loose his hand and cut off my life! ¹⁰ Then I would still have this consolation— my joy in unrelenting pain— that I had not denied the words of the Holy One. ¹¹ "What strength do I have, that I should still hope? What prospects, that I should be patient? ¹² Do I have the strength of stone? Is my flesh bronze? ¹³ Do I have any power to help myself, now that success has been driven from me? ¹¹ "Anyone who withholds kindness from a friend forsakes the fear of the Almighty. ¹⁵ But my brothers are as undependable as intermittent streams, as the streams that overflow ¹⁶ when darkened by thawing ice and swollen with melting snow, ¹⁷ but that stop flowing in the dry season, and in the heat vanish from their channels. [18] Caravans turn aside from their routes; they go off into the wasteland and perish. [19] The caravans of Tema look for water, the traveling merchants of Sheba look in hope. [20] They are distressed, because they had been confident; they arrive there, only to be disappointed. [21] Now you too have proved to be of no help, you see something dreadful and are afraid. [22] Have I ever said, 'Give something on my behalf, pay a ransom for me from your wealth, [23] deliver me from the hand of the enemy, rescue me from the clutches of the ruthless'? [24] "Teach me, and I will be quiet; show me where I have been wrong. [25] How painful are honest words! But what do your arguments prove? [26] Do you mean to correct what I say, and treat my desperate words as wind? [27] You would even cast lots for the fatherless and barter away your friend. [28] "But now be so kind as to look at me. Would I lie to your face? [29] Relent, do not be unjust; reconsider, for my integrity is at stake. [30] Is there any wickedness on my lips? Can my mouth not discern malice?

Chapter 7 Job Continues

"Do not mortals have hard service on earth? Are not their days like those of hired laborers? [2] Like a slave longing for the evening shadows, or a hired laborer waiting to be paid, [3] so I have been allotted months of futility, and nights of misery have been assigned to me. [4] When I lie down I think, 'How long before I get up?' The night drags on, and I toss and turn until dawn. [5] My body is clothed with worms and scabs, my skin is broken and festering. [6] "My days are swifter than a weaver's shuttle, and they come to an end without hope. [7] Remember, O God, that my life is but a breath; my eyes will never see

happiness again. ⁸ *The eye that now sees me will see me no longer; you will look for me, but I will be no more.* ⁹ *As a cloud vanishes and is gone, so one who goes down to the grave does not return.* ¹⁰ *He will never come to his house again; his place will know him no more.* ¹¹ *"Therefore I will not keep silent; I will speak out in the anguish of my spirit, I will complain in the bitterness of my soul.* ¹² *Am I the sea, or the monster of the deep, that you put me under guard?* ¹³ *When I think my bed will comfort me and my couch will ease my complaint,* ¹⁴ *even then you frighten me with dreams and terrify me with visions,* ¹⁵ *so that I prefer strangling and death, rather than this body of mine.* ¹⁶ *I despise my life; I would not live forever. Let me alone; my days have no meaning.* ¹⁷ *"What is mankind that you make so much of them, that you give them so much attention,* ¹⁸ *that you examine them every morning and test them every moment?* ¹⁹ *Will you never look away from me, or let me alone even for an instant?* ²⁰ *If I have sinned, what have I done to you, you who see everything we do? Why have you made me your target? Have I become a burden to you?* ²¹ *Why do you not pardon my offenses and forgive my sins? For I will soon lie down in the dust; you will search for me, but I will be no more."*

In Chapter Six, Job begins by focusing on his misery. To illustrate the intensity of his mental, emotional, and physical anguish, he proclaims it is greater than the sand on the seas. He insists God has shot poisonous arrows at him and his spirit is drinking the poison. He continues to ask for his desire to be granted: the ending of his life. He questions his own strength and knows he is powerless to help himself.

Then, his attention turns to his friends. He declares to his friends that one who is not kind to a friend "forsakes the fear of the Almighty" (v. 14). He says his brothers are undependable, and he compares them to streams which are intermittent (inconsistent), overflowing when blocked by ice and snow, and those that stop flowing in various seasons (unreliable).

Job's claim is his friends are fearful because of what they see (Job's condition) and as a result, they are of no help. He demands to know if he had ever asked for assistance from any of them before. He cries out earnestly to them to show him where he is wrong in the situation, and he questions how they can disregard his words. He closes by asking them to look at him and demands to know if they believe he would lie to their faces about his actions. He implores them greatly because his integrity is at stake.

In Chapter Seven, Job continues with his lament. He makes it known that his life is presumably over, so he states in verse eleven, *"Therefore I will not keep silent; I will speak out in the anguish of my spirit, I will complain in the bitterness of my soul."* He has now turned his attention to God. He asks God, *"Will you never look away from me, or let me alone even for an instant? If I have sinned, what have I done to you, you who see everything we do? Why have you made me your target? Have I become a burden to you? Why do you not pardon my offenses and forgive my sins? For I will soon lie down in the dust; you will search for me, but I will be no more"* (v. 19-21).

Job is well aware God is in control. He asks God to point out his sin. Job clearly is grasping for understanding of what wrong he may have done towards God that would warrant such undertakings.

As you read the above passages, did Job's concerns regarding his friends' reaction towards him resonate with you?

His words resounded loudly in my mind. I could almost literally hear him cry out in agony to his friends. Can you imagine going through a trial and the people you desire and expect to be by your side are not? Imagine how many people in our churches suffer in this very manner. It is very possible that we have all been guilty of this at some time or another.

Just the other day, I heard someone say, "If a person is afflicted with something, it is because of something the person has done and he needs to examine his life to find out what is was." To make sure I heard the person clearly, I repeated what was said by asking, "Are you saying when a person is afflicted it is because of a sin the person committed?" The respondent said, "Yes. See, people want to make everyone believe they are living holy, but that's just an act."

I was intrigued while yet horrified by the inaccuracy of the person's standpoint. I offered a correction by stating, "The Bible says sin entered the world by one man. Therefore, due to the existence of sin in the Earth realm, everyone can fall victim to evil whether or not the person is engaged in sin." For good measure and to drive my point home, I added, "What about the baby who is born blind or crippled? Should he examine his life to see what sin he as committed?" With those questions, I ended the conversation, leaving the person with her own thoughts to ponder and consider the Word of God.

Oftentimes when one is looking for the comfort of another fleshly being, he is often disappointed. Job's friend Elaphaz rebuked him when he requested death to come and relieve him of his suffering. This did not deter Job who was looking for relief. He again made his request known for death to come and free him from agony.

Chapter Six
Then Comes Another

Chapter 8 Bildad

Then Bildad the Shuhite replied: [2] "How long will you say such things? Your words are a blustering wind. [3] Does God pervert justice? Does the Almighty pervert what is right? [4] When your children sinned against him, he gave them over to the penalty of their sin. [5] But if you will seek God earnestly and plead with the Almighty, [6] if you are pure and upright, even now he will rouse himself on your behalf and restore you to your prosperous state. [7] Your beginnings will seem humble, so prosperous will your future be. [8] "Ask the former generation and find out what their ancestors learned, [9] for we were born only yesterday and know nothing, and our days on earth are but a shadow. [10] Will they not instruct you and tell you? Will they not bring forth words from their understanding? [11] Can papyrus grow tall where there is no marsh? Can reeds thrive without water? [12] While still growing and uncut, they wither more quickly than grass. [13] Such is the destiny of all who forget God; so perishes the hope of the godless. [14] What they trust in is fragile; what they rely on is a spider's web. [15] They lean on the web, but it gives way; they cling to it, but it does not hold. [16] They are like a well-watered plant in the sunshine, spreading its shoots over the garden; [17] it entwines its roots around a pile of rocks and looks for a place among the stones. ¹⁸ But when it is torn from its spot, that place disowns it and says, 'I never saw you.' ¹⁹ Surely its life withers away, and from the soil other plants grow. ²⁰ "Surely God does not reject one who is blameless or strengthen the hands of evildoers. ²¹ He will yet fill your mouth with laughter and your lips with shouts of joy. ²² Your enemies will be clothed in shame, and the tents of the wicked will be no more."

In this chapter, another of Job's visiting friends decides it is his turn to reflect on Job's situation. Before he fully engages in his discourse, he first attempts to quiet Job by asking, *"How long will you say such things? Your words are a blustering wind"* (v. 2). That is to say, Job's voice was turbulent and bothersome like a loud noisy wind that comes in suddenly and unexpectedly.

Bildad continues his discourse by telling Job how just God is. He makes his statement clear by bringing up Job's children and using them as an example of how God's actions are just. He states that Job's children's lives were taken because of their sinful living. But, he assures Job if he is blameless, he will not suffer the same fate. Bildad believes all Job had lost would be restored unto him and what he had in the beginning will appear humble to how God would bless him.

Continuing to offer advice, Bildad tells Job to consult the former generations for advice because they are older, have more experience, and are more knowledgeable about God. Comparatively speaking, Job and his friends are novices. Bildad insists those who fail to be strengthened by God will fall. But God will not reject a blameless person. Instead, he will be filled with laughter and joy. His enemies will be shamed and the wicked will be destroyed.

Bildad is reassuring Job if he is 'just' as he proclaims, he has nothing to worry about because God will not forsake him.

As a word of caution when dealing with our brethren:
> May we choose the portion, possess the confidence, bear the cross, and die the death of the righteous; and, in the meantime, be careful neither to wound others by rash judgments, nor to distress ourselves needlessly about the opinions of our fellow-creatures. (Henry, 2014)

The Bottom Line

Chapter Seven
Allow Me to Respond

Chapter 9 Job

Then Job replied: ² "Indeed, I know that this is true. But how can mere mortals prove their innocence before God? ³ Though they wished to dispute with him, they could not answer him one time out of a thousand. ⁴ His wisdom is profound, his power is vast. Who has resisted him and come out unscathed. ⁵ He moves mountains without their knowing it and overturns them in his anger. ⁶ He shakes the earth from its place and makes its pillars tremble. ⁷ He speaks to the sun and it does not shine; he seals off the light of the stars. ⁸ He alone stretches out the heavens and treads on the waves of the sea. ⁹ He is the Maker of the Bear and Orion, the Pleiades and the constellations of the south. ¹⁰ He performs wonders that cannot be fathomed, miracles that cannot be counted. ¹¹ When he passes me, I cannot see him; when he goes by, I cannot perceive him. ¹² If he snatches away, who can stop him? Who can say to him, 'What are you doing?' ¹³ God does not restrain his anger; even the cohorts of Rahab cowered at his feet. ¹⁴ "How then can I dispute with him? How can I find words to argue with him? ¹⁵ Though I were innocent, I could not answer him; I could only plead with my Judge for mercy. ¹⁶ Even if I summoned him and he responded, I do not believe he would give me a hearing.

17 He would crush me with a storm and multiply my wounds for no reason. *18* He would not let me catch my breath but would overwhelm me with misery. *19* If it is a matter of strength, he is mighty! And if it is a matter of justice, who can challenge him? *20* Even if I were innocent, my mouth would condemn me; if I were blameless, it would pronounce me guilty. *21* "Although I am blameless, I have no concern for myself; I despise my own life. *22* It is all the same; that is why I say, 'He destroys both the blameless and the wicked.' *23* When a scourge brings sudden death, he mocks the despair of the innocent. *24* When a land falls into the hands of the wicked, he blindfolds its judges. If it is not he, then who is it? *25* "My days are swifter than a runner; they fly away without a glimpse of joy. *26* They skim past like boats of papyrus, like eagles swooping down on their prey. *27* If I say, 'I will forget my complaint, I will change my expression, and smile,' *28* I still dread all my sufferings, for I know you will not hold me innocent. *29* Since I am already found guilty, why should I struggle in vain? *30* Even if I washed myself with soap and my hands with cleansing powder, *31* you would plunge me into a slime pit so that even my clothes would detest me. *32* "He is not a mere mortal like me that I might answer him, that we might confront each other in court. *33* If only there were someone to mediate between us, someone to bring us together, *34* someone to remove God's rod from me, so that his terror would frighten me no more. *35* Then I would speak up without fear of him, but as it now stands with me, I cannot.*

Job agrees with Bildad's statements, but he asks, *"How can mere mortals prove their innocence before God?"* (v. 2b). Before allowing Bildad an opportunity to respond, Job continues to provide God's extensive resume, demonstrating His vastness, omnipresence, and omnipotence.

Job says even being innocent he cannot argue with God. His only recourse is pleading for God's mercy. But, Job does not believe God would hear his case. Instead, he believes God would, *"crush [him] with a storm and multiply [his] wounds for no reason. He would not let [him] catch [his] breath but would overwhelm [him] with misery"* (v. 17-18).

Job also believes his own mouth would betray him by condemning him and proclaiming his guilt. Therefore he contends, *"He destroys both the blameless and the wicked"* (v. 22b). Job insists because God is not a mere mortal, he and God are unequal, so he cannot stand up against God. In verses 33-35, Job says, *"If only there were someone to mediate between us, someone to bring us together, someone to remove God's rod from me, so that his terror would frighten me no more. Then I would speak up without fear of him, but as it now stands with me, I cannot."*

In all Job had said, he acknowledged God's power and sovereignty. He believed he could not speak up for himself because he would suffer more of God's wrath for doing so. He was terrified of God's hand, and he desired an intermediary but did not know of one who could intercede on his behalf.

Today, believers have the same reverence for God. We understand His sovereignty, His omniscience, His omnipotence, and His omnipresence. We have an undying love for God, and we know He has an everlasting love for us. He loves us so much that He sent His only begotten son to save us from the penalty of sin.

Romans 6:23 states, *"For the wages of sin is death, but the gift of God is eternal life in Christ Jesus our Lord."* In order for us to escape death, Jesus came to take upon Himself the punishment that was rightfully ours. After suffering death by crucifixion, Jesus eventually ascended back to heaven, taking a seat on the right hand of the Father (Luke 22:69). Now, Jesus makes intercessions for us (Romans 8:34).

When we are faced with trials and adversities, we can pray to Jesus and make our requests known. He then goes to the Father on our behalf. He is our high priest, and we have direct access to Him.

Chapter Eight
Flowing Like a River

Chapter 10 Job

"I loathe my very life; therefore I will give free rein to my complaint and speak out in the bitterness of my soul. ² I say to God: Do not declare me guilty, but tell me what charges you have against me. ³ Does it please you to oppress me, to spurn the work of your hands, while you smile on the plans of the wicked? ⁴ Do you have eyes of flesh? Do you see as a mortal sees? ⁵ Are your days like those of a mortal or your years like those of a strong man, ⁶ that you must search out my faults and probe after my sin ⁷ though you know that I am not guilty and that no one can rescue me from your hand? ⁸ "Your hands shaped me and made me. Will you now turn and destroy me? ⁹ Remember that you molded me like clay. Will you now turn me to dust again? ¹⁰ Did you not pour me out like milk and curdle me like cheese, ¹¹ clothe me with skin and flesh and knit me together with bones and sinews? ¹² You gave me life and showed me kindness, and in your providence watched over my spirit. ¹³ "But this is what you concealed in your heart, and I know that this was in your mind: ¹⁴ If I sinned, you would be watching me and would not let my offense go unpunished. ¹⁵ If I am guilty—woe to me! Even if I am innocent, I cannot lift my head, for I am full of shame and drowned in my affliction. ¹⁶ If I

hold my head high, you stalk me like a lion and again display your awesome power against me. ^{17} *You bring new witnesses against me and increase your anger toward me; your forces come against me wave upon wave.* ^{18} *"Why then did you bring me out of the womb? I wish I had died before any eye saw me.* ^{19} *If only I had never come into being, or had been carried straight from the womb to the grave!* ^{20} *Are not my few days almost over? Turn away from me so I can have a moment's joy* ^{21} *before I go to the place of no return, to the land of gloom and utter darkness,* ^{22} *to the land of deepest night, of utter darkness and disorder, where even the light is like darkness."*

Job's discourse from Chapter 9 continues on into Chapter 10. Due to the extreme circumstances Job was experiencing, his belly is full and his lament flows like living waters, from a brook that has no end. He is still attempting to understand why he is being tormented. He finds no fault within himself and does not believe God does either.

In this chapter, we find Job's attention is no longer on his friends but continues to focus on God and His supposed wrath. He asks if the hands that fashioned him will now destroy him. He talks about good God has been to him but then he suddenly declares how God has concealed in His heart what He would do if Job had sinned. He accuses God of bringing witnesses against him and rising up in anger. All of Job's thoughts and outbursts bring him to a question, *"Why then did you bring me out of the womb?"* (v. 18).

Obviously, Job feels it would have been better if he had never been born. He cannot fathom why he would be born to face such turmoil. He cannot wrap his human mind around the concept. In closing, Job pleads with God for one moment of pleasure or relief before he departs the earth.

Have you ever faced a situation that left you angry at God or confused? If so, how did you deal with it? Did you find yourself being angrier and angrier at God as you tried desperately to understand His reasons for allowing the situation to happen?

One question believers have struggled with and continue to struggle with is, "Why do bad things happen to good people?" The first question I would ask as a reply is, "What person do you know who is inherently good?" Romans 7:18 says, *"For I know that good itself does not dwell in me, that is, in my sinful nature. For I have the desire to do what is good, but I cannot carry it out."*

The Bible also says we were born in sin and shaped in iniquity (Psalm 51:5). Therefore, there isn't anything good within us. Also, the Bible says all have sinned and fall short of the glory of God (Romans 3:23). So, when we ask, "Why do bad things happen to good people?" what we are really asking is why do bad things happen to people who have a loving spirit and try to live according to the statutes of God.

Well, bad things happen to all people because of the sinful state the world is in. Satan, who is the prince of the power of the air, has a measure of power, and because of our disobedience to God, we fall victim to Satan- with God's permission of course, and for a reason of course. By 'our disobedience to God' I am not referring to our individual sin. Rather, I am referring to the overall sin of mankind.

The Bottom Line

As I stated in the introduction, there is a reason for everything that occurs in our lives. Nothing happens by happenstance. There is a **bottom line** to each and everything we go through. It is just up to us to figure it out!

Chapter Nine
No Punches Withheld

Chapter 11 Zophar

Then Zophar the Naamathite replied: ² "Are all these words to go unanswered? Is this talker to be vindicated? ³ Will your idle talk reduce others to silence? Will no one rebuke you when you mock? ⁴ You say to God, 'My beliefs are flawless and I am pure in your sight.' ⁵ Oh, how I wish that God would speak, that he would open his lips against you ⁶ and disclose to you the secrets of wisdom, for true wisdom has two sides. Know this: God has even forgotten some of your sin. ⁷ "Can you fathom the mysteries of God? Can you probe the limits of the Almighty? ⁸ They are higher than the heavens above—what can you do? They are deeper than the depths below—what can you know? ⁹ Their measure is longer than the earth and wider than the sea. ¹⁰ "If he comes along and confines you in prison and convenes a court, who can oppose him? ¹¹ Surely he recognizes deceivers; and when he sees evil, does he not take note? ¹² But the witless can no more become wise than a wild donkey's colt can be born human. ¹³ "Yet if you devote your heart to him and stretch out your hands to him, ¹⁴ if you put away the sin that is in your hand and allow no evil to dwell in your tent, ¹⁵ then, free of fault, you will lift up your face; you will stand firm and without fear. ¹⁶ You will surely forget your trouble, recalling it only as waters gone by. ¹⁷ Life will be brighter than noonday, and darkness will become like morning. ¹⁸ You will be secure, because there is hope; you will look about you and take your rest in safety. ¹⁹ You will lie down, with no one to make you afraid, and many will court your favor. ²⁰ But the eyes of the wicked will fail, and escape will elude them; their hope will become a dying gasp."

Zophar holds no punches; he immediately reveals to Job his take on the words Job spouted out at God. Zophar does not believe God will remain silent after Job's rant. Even more so, Zophar hopes God doesn't stay silent. He says in verse five, *"Oh, how I wish that God would speak, that he would open his lips against you."*

Zophar then begins to demonstrate for Job how he is no match for God, so how dare he address God the way he did. Zophar finds Job to be very disrespectful. With example after example, Zophar aims to show Job how foolish he is to question God in the accusatory tone he used.

Zophar continues by telling Job if he is truly innocent as he professes, he would lift his face and stand firm without fear. He tells him he would forget his trouble, and he would be secure because of the hope he would possess. Zophar closes his rebuke with a thought: *"But the eyes of the wicked will fail, and escape will elude them; their hope will become a dying gasp"* (v. 20).

Perhaps, Zophar closes with these words because he wants to exhibit his feelings about Job's position. Despite Job's plea of innocence, Zophar does not believe him. He has determined Job's current actions speak the truth about Job's situation.

Zophar exhorts Job to repentance and gives him encouragement, yet mixed with hard thoughts of him. He thought that worldly prosperity was always the lot of the righteous, and that Job was to be deemed a hypocrite unless his prosperity was restored. Then shalt thou lift up thy face without spot; that is, thou mayst come boldly to the throne of grace, and not with the terror and amazement expressed in Ch. 9:34. If we are looked upon in the face of the Anointed, our faces that were cast down may be lifted up; though polluted, being now washed with the blood of Christ, they may be lifted up without spot. We may draw near in full assurance of faith, when we are sprinkled from an evil conscience, Heb. 10:22. (Henry, 2014)

The Bottom Line

Chapter Ten
Knowledge Reigns Supreme

Chapter 12 Job

Then Job replied: ² "Doubtless you are the only people who matter, and wisdom will die with you! ³ But I have a mind as well as you; I am not inferior to you. Who does not know all these things? ⁴ "I have become a laughingstock to my friends, though I called on God and he answered— a mere laughingstock, though righteous and blameless! ⁵ Those who are at ease have contempt for misfortune as the fate of those whose feet are slipping. ⁶ The tents of marauders are undisturbed, and those who provoke God are secure— those God has in his hand. ⁷ "But ask the animals, and they will teach you, or the birds in the sky, and they will tell you; ⁸ or speak to the earth, and it will teach you, or let the fish in the sea inform you. ⁹ Which of all these does not know that the hand of the LORD has done this? ¹⁰ In his hand is the life of every creature and the breath of all mankind. ¹¹ Does not the ear test words as the tongue tastes food? ¹² Is not wisdom found among the aged? Does not long life bring understanding? ¹³ "To God belong wisdom and power; counsel and understanding are his. ¹⁴ What he tears down cannot be rebuilt; those he imprisons cannot be released. ¹⁵ If he holds back the waters, there is drought; if he lets them loose, they devastate the land. ⁱ⁶ To him belong strength and insight; both deceived and deceivers are his. ¹⁷ He leads rulers away stripped and makes fools of judges. ¹⁸ He takes off the shackles put on by kings and ties a loincloth around their waist. ¹⁹ He leads priests away stripped and overthrows officials long established. ²⁰ He silences the lips of trusted advisers and takes away the discernment of elders. ²¹ He pours contempt on nobles and disarms the mighty. ²² He reveals the deep things of darkness and brings utter darkness into the light. ²³ He makes nations great, and destroys them; he enlarges nations, and disperses them. ²⁴ He deprives the leaders of the earth of their reason; he makes them wander in a trackless waste. ²⁵ They grope in darkness with no light; he makes them stagger like drunkards.

Just as Zophar wasted no time in getting to his point, Job does not waste time or mince words when it comes to responding to Zophar's position. The friends (including Job) do not hesitate to ridicule one another with the perceptions they presently hold.

Job informs Zophar that he, Eliphaz, and Bildad are not the only ones whose opinions matter and they are not the holders of all wisdom. He immediately attempts to level the playing field by letting them know he can think as well as they can, and they are not superior to him. He assures them he knows all they have attempted to share with him.

Going further, Job lets them know he knows his friends are laughing at him while he suffers at God's hands. He makes it plain with use of many examples that God is in full control of the universe and every creature knows it. Therefore, Job perceives it is God who has brought the suffering to him.

All the examples of God's sovereignty Job included in his response reveal truths about God.

These important truths were suited to convince the disputants that they were out of their depth in attempting to assign the Lord's reasons for afflicting Job; his ways are unsearchable, and his judgments past finding out. Let us remark what beautiful illustrations there are in the word of God, confirming his sovereignty, and wisdom in that sovereignty: but the highest and infinitely the most important is, that the Lord Jesus was crucified by the malice of the Jews; and who but the Lord could have known that this one event was the salvation of the world? (Henry, 2014)

Chapter 13 Job Continues

"My eyes have seen all this, my ears have heard and understood it. ^{2} What you know, I also know; I am not inferior to you. ^{3} But I desire to speak to the Almighty and to argue my case with God. ^{4} You, however, smear me with lies; you are worthless physicians, all of you! ^{5} If only you would be altogether silent! For you, that would be wisdom. ^{6} Hear now my argument; listen to the pleas of my lips. ^{7} Will you speak wickedly on God's behalf? Will you speak deceitfully for him? ^{8} Will you show him partiality? Will you argue the case for God? ^{9} Would it turn out well if he examined you? Could you deceive him as you might deceive a mortal? ^{10} He would surely call you to account if you secretly showed partiality. ^{11} Would

not his splendor terrify you? Would not the dread of him fall on you? ⁱ² Your maxims are proverbs of ashes; your defenses are defenses of clay. ¹³ "Keep silent and let me speak; then let come to me what may. ¹⁴ Why do I put myself in jeopardy and take my life in my hands? ¹⁵ Though he slay me, yet will I hope in him; I will surely defend my ways to his face. ¹⁶ Indeed, this will turn out for my deliverance, for no godless person would dare come before him! ¹⁷ Listen carefully to what I say; let my words ring in your ears. ¹⁸ Now that I have prepared my case, I know I will be vindicated. ¹⁹ Can anyone bring charges against me? If so, I will be silent and die. ²⁰ "Only grant me these two things, God, and then I will not hide from you: ²¹ Withdraw your hand far from me, and stop frightening me with your terrors. ²² Then summon me and I will answer, or let me speak, and you reply to me. ²³ How many wrongs and sins have I committed? Show me my offense and my sin. ²⁴ Why do you hide your face and consider me your enemy? ²⁵ Will you torment a windblown leaf? Will you chase after dry chaff? ²⁶ For you write down bitter things against me and make me reap the sins of my youth. ²⁷ You fasten my feet in shackles; you keep close watch on all my paths by putting marks on the soles of my feet. ²⁸ "So man wastes away like something rotten, like a garment eaten by moths.

Job continues his discourse and reminds his friends that he is not inferior to them as he holds the same information as they do. He then agrees with their assertions of him crying out and questioning God. He admits he spoke out to God and says it was simply to reason with Him. He says they, on the other hand, tell lies instead of offering comfort to him, a friend in distress.

He continues by telling them it would be wise of them to hold their peace and remain quiet while he provides his reasons for his actions to them. He then assertively asks his friends if they boldly speak on God's behalf. He reproves them for not having the proper reverence for God. He implores them to leave him alone to speak his mind and whatever may befall him as a result, let it be. He says even if God slays him, he will continue to trust in Him. After speaking to his friends, Job turns his attention to God and asks for two things: He depended upon God for justification and salvation.

Of his eternal salvation, [Job] was very confident; that God would not only be his Saviour to make him happy, but his salvation, in the sight and enjoyment of whom he should be happy. He knew himself not to be a hypocrite, and concluded that he should not be rejected. (Henry, 2014)

Chapter 14 Job Continues

"Mortals, born of woman, are of few days and full of trouble. ² They spring up like flowers and wither away; like fleeting shadows, they do not endure. ³ Do you fix your eye on them? Will you bring them before you for judgment? ⁴ Who can bring what is pure from the impure? No one! ⁵ A person's days are determined; you have decreed the number of his months and have set limits he cannot exceed. ⁶ So look away from him and let him alone, till he has put in his time like a hired laborer. ⁷ "At least there is hope for a tree: If it is cut down, it will sprout again, and its new shoots will not fail. ⁸ Its roots may grow old in the ground and its stump die in the soil, ⁹ yet at the

scent of water it will bud and put forth shoots like a plant. [10] But a man dies and is laid low; he breathes his last and is no more. [11] As the water of a lake dries up or a riverbed becomes parched and dry, [12] so he lies down and does not rise; till the heavens are no more, people will not awake or be roused from their sleep. [13] "If only you would hide me in the grave and conceal me till your anger has passed! If only you would set me a time and then remember me! [14] If someone dies, will they live again? All the days of my hard service I will wait for my renewal to come. [15] You will call and I will answer you; you will long for the creature your hands have made. [16] Surely then you will count my steps but not keep track of my sin. [17] My offenses will be sealed up in a bag; you will cover over my sin. [18] "But as a mountain erodes and crumbles and as a rock is moved from its place, [19] as water wears away stones and torrents wash away the soil, so you destroy a person's hope. [20] You overpower them once for all, and they are gone; you change their countenance and send them away. [21] If their children are honored, they do not know it; if their offspring are brought low, they do not see it. [22] They feel but the pain of their own bodies and mourn only for themselves."

Job reflects on what it means to be human. He describes human life as being fragile and imperfect, as humans are imperfect beings. He asks if something pure can come from something impure. This statement appears to refer back to the original sin of Adam. Because of Adam's sin, mankind from that point forward was born in sin. Therefore, the answer to Job's question is automatically- No.

Then, Job turned his focus to God as the creator and the ruler of the universe. He talks about man's days being numbered because God has limited the number of days we will spend on this earth. He then implores God to leave man alone until his days on Earth come to an end and not to cause him suffering.

By way of examples and comparisons to other living organisms, Job compares man's life and demonstrates how man's death is permanent. He knows God will cover his sin, but he contends God overpowers man. This discourse if filled with agony mixed with hope. The small ray of hope is quickly diminished by the agonizing pathos demonstrated by Job.

Notice how Job, in his complete emotion-filled response, does not once bring up the name of the adversary- Satan. Instead, he illustrates the good and the bad that can befall humans, and he says it is all due to a sovereign god. Is he right? Of course, he is! God is all powerful, and He and only He is in full control! However, Job must understand that sickness, disease and calamity do not come directly from God. God permits these things to happen, but they are done from the hand of our adversary.

Question- Is the question- "Who is in control of what Job experienced?" No! That is not the question at all. That answer is readily apparent. Well then, what is the question? The question that should be asked is, "*Why* did calamity befall Job?"

By asking this question, we are desirous to know and understand the bottom line of Job's situation. Continue reading as we work toward that end.

The Bottom Line

At this point, we have only covered fourteen chapters. There are twenty-eight more to go. Let us keep plugging away.

Chapter Eleven
Fiery Darts

Chapter 15 Eliphaz

"Then Eliphaz the Temanite replied: ² "Would a wise person answer with empty notions or fill their belly with the hot east wind? ³ Would they argue with useless words, with speeches that have no value? ⁴ But you even undermine piety and hinder devotion to God. ⁵ Your sin prompts your mouth; you adopt the tongue of the crafty. ⁶ Your own mouth condemns you, not mine; your own lips testify against you. ⁷ "Are you the first man ever born? Were you brought forth before the hills? ⁸ Do you listen in on God's council? Do you have a monopoly on wisdom? ⁹ What do you know that we do not know? What insights do you have that we do not have? ¹⁰ The gray-haired and the aged are on our side, men even older than your father. ¹¹ Are God's consolations not enough for you, words spoken gently to you? ¹² Why has your heart carried you away, and why do your eyes flash, ¹³ so that you vent your rage against God and pour out such words from your mouth? ¹⁴ "What are mortals, that they could be pure, or those born of woman, that they could be righteous? ¹⁵ If God places no trust in his holy ones, if even the heavens are not pure in his eyes, ¹⁶ how much less mortals, who are vile and corrupt, who drink up evil like water! ¹⁷ "Listen to me and I will explain to you; let me tell you

what I have seen, ^{18} what the wise have declared, hiding nothing received from their ancestors ^{19} (to whom alone the land was given when no foreigners moved among them): ^{20} All his days the wicked man suffers torment, the ruthless man through all the years stored up for him. ^{21} Terrifying sounds fill his ears; when all seems well, marauders attack him. ^{22} He despairs of escaping the realm of darkness; he is marked for the sword. ^{23} He wanders about for food like a vulture; he knows the day of darkness is at hand. ^{24} Distress and anguish fill him with terror; troubles overwhelm him, like a king poised to attack, ^{25} because he shakes his fist at God and vaunts himself against the Almighty, ^{26} defiantly charging against him with a thick, strong shield. ^{27} "Though his face is covered with fat and his waist bulges with flesh, ^{28} he will inhabit ruined towns and houses where no one lives, houses crumbling to rubble. ^{29} He will no longer be rich and his wealth will not endure, nor will his possessions spread over the land. ^{30} He will not escape the darkness; a flame will wither his shoots, and the breath of God's mouth will carry him away. ^{31} Let him not deceive himself by trusting what is worthless, for he will get nothing in return. ^{32} Before his time he will wither, and his branches will not flourish. ^{33} He will be like a vine stripped of its unripe grapes, like an olive tree shedding its blossoms. ^{34} For the company of the godless will be barren, and fire will consume the tents of those who love bribes. ^{35} They conceive trouble and give birth to evil; their womb fashions deceit."

Eliphaz really lays into Job with a harsh rebuke, as a defense for himself and their two friends. He discounts all Job has said by asking him if he was the first born of all and if he had insight to God's desires and plans. Basically, he is asking Job how he presumes to know what God is thinking and what His plans are. Eliphaz continues his harsh rebuke by telling Job his mouth has turned against him and he does not know as much as he professes to know. He questions God's consolations for Job. Based on Job's behaviors and words, Eliphaz determines Job finds them insufficient because he has seemingly turned his mouth against God with his vile words.

Then, Eliphaz raises a good question- "If God does not put trust in the heavenly hosts, why would He do so in man who is sinful and corrupt?" He proceeds to answer his own question by telling Job what he knows from what he has seen with his own eyes and what he has heard from wise men. His answer encompasses many examples from the troubled life man lives when he has not chosen to trust God; it is a life of problems, deceit, and wickedness.

From Eliphaz's perspective, Job sounds like a man who has lost his devotion to God and has ventured out on his own. In doing so, he has become lifted up in himself and has turned away from the Almighty. Eliphaz's rebuke is meant to talk some sense into Job because from Eliphaz's perspective, Job has lost his trust in God and only looks to himself for answers.

So far in fifteen chapters, we have witnessed controversial perspectives shared between Job and his friends. Job suffered great losses and his friends, having heard, come to his aid. At least, that is what one would expect from friends. And, our expectations seem to be on the right track when we witness in the reading, *"When Job's three friends, Eliphaz the Temanite, Bildad the Shuhite and Zophar the Naamathite, heard about all* the troubles that had come upon him, they set out from their homes and met together by agreement to go and sympathize with him and comfort him. When they saw him from a distance, they could hardly recognize him; they began to weep aloud, and they tore their robes and sprinkled dust on their heads. Then they sat on the ground with him for seven days and seven nights. No one said a word to him, because they saw how great his suffering was"* (1:11-13).

However, after the seven days of silence that was demonstrative of a mourning period, the tables turned toward the unexpected. In Chapter 1, Job was described as a *"man [who] was blameless and upright; he feared God and shunned evil"*(v. 1b). Who would have thought he would utter words towards God as he did? And to add to our confusion, Job's friends utter words that are like daggers of ridicule and contempt.

Let's continue to survey the Book of Job and see what unfolds in the life of Job!

Chapter Twelve
Woe is Me!

Chapter 16 Job

Then Job replied: [2] "I have heard many things like these; you are miserable comforters, all of you! [3] Will your long-winded speeches never end? What ails you that you keep on arguing? [4] I also could speak like you, if you were in my place; I could make fine speeches against you and shake my head at you. [5] But my mouth would encourage you; comfort from my lips would bring you relief. [6] "Yet if I speak, my pain is not relieved; and if I refrain, it does not go away. [7] Surely, God, you have worn me out; you have devastated my entire household. [8] You have shriveled me up—and it has become a witness; my gauntness rises up and testifies against me. [9] God assails me and tears me in his anger and gnashes his teeth at me; my opponent fastens on me his piercing eyes. [10] People open their mouths to jeer at me; they strike my cheek in scorn and unite together against me. [11] God has turned me over to the ungodly and thrown me into the clutches of the wicked. [12] All was well with me, but he shattered me; he seized me by the neck and crushed me. He has made me his target; [13] his archers surround me. Without pity, he pierces my kidneys and spills my gall on the ground. [14] Again and again he bursts upon me; he rushes at me like a warrior. [15] "I have sewed sackcloth over my skin and buried my brow in the dust. [16] *My face is red with weeping, dark shadows ring my eyes;* [17] *yet my hands have been free of violence and my prayer is pure.* [18] *"Earth, do not cover my blood; may my cry never be laid to rest!* [19] *Even now my witness is in heaven; my advocate is on high.* [20] *My intercessor is my friend as my eyes pour out tears to God;* [21] *on behalf of a man he pleads with God as one pleads for a friend.* [22] *"Only a few years will pass before I take the path of no return.*

Chapter 17 Job Continues

My spirit is broken, my days are cut short, the grave awaits me. [2] *Surely mockers surround me; my eyes must dwell on their hostility.* [3] *"Give me, O God, the pledge you demand. Who else will put up security for me?* [4] *You have closed their minds to understanding; therefore you will not let them triumph.* [5] *If anyone denounces their friends for reward, the eyes of their children will fail.* [6] *"God has made me a byword to everyone, a man in whose face people spit.* [7] *My eyes have grown dim with grief; my whole frame is but a shadow.* [8] *The upright are appalled at this; the innocent are aroused against the ungodly.* [9] *Nevertheless, the righteous will hold to their ways, and those with clean hands will grow stronger.* [10] *"But come on, all of you, try again! I will not find a wise man among you.* [11] *My days have passed, my plans are shattered. Yet the desires of my heart* [12] *turn night into day; in the face of the darkness light is near.* [13] *If the only home I hope for is the grave, if I spread out my bed in the realm of darkness,* [14] *if I say to corruption, 'You are my father,' and to the worm, 'My mother' or 'My sister,'* [15] *where then is my hope—who can see any hope for me?*

¹⁶ *Will it go down to the gates of death? Will we descend together into the dust?"*

Job has had as much as he can take from the tongues of his friends. He fails to understand why each of his friend's monologues persist when they only deliver more pain. As he stated earlier, as friends, they aren't doing well in the comforting department. He tells them if he were in their positions, he too could speak as they do with fine speeches that condemn. However, Job makes it clear he would speak words of comfort rather than words of condemnation. He informs them that their own words bring him no comfort or relief. Then, he begins to speak to God and declares the impact of the devastation in his life and how the wounds deepen when those around him stand in ridicule. He states all was well with him, but God seized him by the neck and tore him apart without mercy. Then, he was thrown to the wicked, and they have done exceeding damage as well.

Job continues to appeal to God for death, so his suffering can come to an end. He tells his friends to continue with their attempts at wisdom, but he assures them, he will not find one wise among them.

In all Job says, he offers wisdom about death. He may be asking for death to end his immediate suffering, but he may also be speaking about death from the standpoint that his life has truly come to an end. He stands fatherless as all his children have perished. Now, he has no one to guide and no one to instruct. He has no servants and no cattle to tend to, so from his perspective his earthly life has ended. Therefore, Job sees no need to remain.

The Bottom Line

But, our days are numbered by God, and we should pray, *"Teach us to number our days, that we may apply our hearts unto wisdom"* (Psalms 90:12, KJV). In doing so, we will wisely use our time that God has graciously given us.

Chapter Thirteen
The Verbal Attacks Continue

Chapter 18 Bildad

Then Bildad the Shuhite replied: ² "When will you end these speeches? Be sensible, and then we can talk. ³ Why are we regarded as cattle and considered stupid in your sight? ⁴ You who tear yourself to pieces in your anger, is the earth to be abandoned for your sake? Or must the rocks be moved from their place? ⁵ "The lamp of a wicked man is snuffed out; the flame of his fire stops burning. ⁶ The light in his tent becomes dark; the lamp beside him goes out. ⁷ The vigor of his step is weakened; his own schemes throw him down. ⁸ His feet thrust him into a net; he wanders into its mesh. ⁹ A trap seizes him by the heel; a snare holds him fast. ¹⁰ A noose is hidden for him on the ground; a trap lies in his path. ¹¹ Terrors startle him on every side and dog his every step. ¹² Calamity is hungry for him; disaster is ready for him when he falls. ¹³ It eats away parts of his skin; death's firstborn devours his limbs. ¹⁴ He is torn from the security of his tent and marched off to the king of terrors. ¹⁵ Fire resides in his tent; burning sulfur is scattered over his dwelling. ¹⁶ His roots dry up below and his branches wither above. ¹⁷ The memory of him perishes from the earth; he has no name in the land. ¹⁸ He is driven from light into the realm of darkness and is banished from the world. ¹⁹ He has no offspring or descendants among his people, no survivor where once he lived. [20] *People of the west are appalled at his fate; those of the east are seized with horror.* [21] *Surely such is the dwelling of an evil man; such is the place of one who does not know God."*

Bildad's outburst to Job demonstrates Satan's attacks. Satan, from the first conversation he had with God, was trying all he could to get Job to turn his back on God. In this chapter, Bildad slings assault after assault, but they are all in vain.

Bildad had before given Job good advice and encouragement; here he used nothing but rebukes, and declared his ruin. And he concluded that Job shut out the providence of God from the management of human affairs, because he would not admit himself to be wicked. Bildad describes the miserable condition of a wicked man; in which there is much certain truth, if we consider that a sinful condition is a sad condition, and that sin will be men's ruin, if they do not repent. Though Bildad thought the application of it to Job was easy, yet it was neither safe nor just.

It is common for angry disputants to rank their opponents among God's enemies, and to draw wrong conclusions from important truths. The destruction of the wicked is foretold. That destruction is represented under the similitude of a beast or bird caught in a snare, or a malefactor taken into custody. Satan, as he was a murderer, so he was a robber, from the beginning. He, the tempter, lays snares for sinners wherever they go. If he makes them sinful like himself, he will make them miserable like himself. Satan hunts for the precious life. In the transgression of an evil man there is a snare for himself, and God is preparing for his destruction. See here how the sinner runs himself into the snare. Bildad describes the destruction wicked people are kept for, in the other world, and which in some degree, often seizes them in this world.

The way of sin is the way of fear, and leads to everlasting confusion, of which the present terrors of an impure conscience are earnests, as in Cain and Judas. Miserable indeed is a wicked man's death, how secure soever his life was. See him dying; all that he trusts to for his support shall be taken from him. How happy are the saints, and how indebted to the lord Jesus, by whom death is so far done away and changed, that this king of terrors is become a friend and a servant! See the wicked man's family sunk and cut off. His children shall perish, either with him or after him. Those who consult the true honour of their family, and its welfare, will be afraid of withering all by sin.

The judgments of God follow the wicked man after death in this world, as a proof of the misery his soul is in after death, and as an earnest of that everlasting shame and contempt to which he shall rise in the great day. The memory of the just is blessed, but the name of the wicked shall rot (Pr. 10:7). It would be well if this report of wicked men would cause any to flee from the wrath to come, from which their power, policy, and riches cannot deliver them.

But Jesus ever liveth to deliver all who trust in him. Bear up then, suffering believers. Ye shall for a little time have sorrow, but your Beloved, your Saviour, will see you again;

your hearts shall rejoice, and your joy no man taketh away. (Henry, 2014)

Chapter Fourteen
Cease and Desist!

Chapter 19 Job

Then Job replied: ^{2} "How long will you torment me and crush me with words? ^{3} Ten times now you have reproached me; shamelessly you attack me. ^{4} If it is true that I have gone astray, my error remains my concern alone. ^{5} If indeed you would exalt yourselves above me and use my humiliation against me, ^{6} then know that God has wronged me and drawn his net around me. ^{7} "Though I cry, 'Violence!' I get no response; though I call for help, there is no justice. ^{8} He has blocked my way so I cannot pass; he has shrouded my paths in darkness. ^{9} He has stripped me of my honor and removed the crown from my head. ^{10} He tears me down on every side till I am gone; he uproots my hope like a tree. ^{11} His anger burns against me; he counts me among his enemies. ^{12} His troops advance in force; they build a siege ramp against me and encamp around my tent. ^{13} "He has alienated my family from me; my acquaintances are completely estranged from me. ^{14} My relatives have gone away; my closest friends have forgotten me. ^{15} My guests and my female servants count me a foreigner; they look on me as on a stranger. ^{16} I summon my servant, but he does not answer, though I beg him with my own mouth. ^{17} My breath is offensive to my wife; I am loathsome to *my own family. ⁱ⁸ Even the little boys scorn me; when I appear, they ridicule me. ¹⁹ All my intimate friends detest me; those I love have turned against me. ²⁰ I am nothing but skin and bones; I have escaped only by the skin of my teeth. ²¹ "Have pity on me, my friends, have pity, for the hand of God has struck me. ²² Why do you pursue me as God does? Will you never get enough of my flesh? ²³ "Oh, that my words were recorded, that they were written on a scroll, ²⁴ that they were inscribed with an iron tool on lead, or engraved in rock forever! ²⁵ I know that my redeemer lives, and that in the end he will stand on the earth. ²⁶ And after my skin has been destroyed, yet in my flesh I will see God; ²⁷ I myself will see him with my own eyes—I, and not another. How my heart yearns within me! ²⁸ "If you say, 'How we will hound him, since the root of the trouble lies in him,' ²⁹ you should fear the sword yourselves; for wrath will bring punishment by the sword, and then you will know that there is judgment."*

Job continues to adamantly proclaim his innocence even when his friends stand in opposition to him. From Job's perspective, God has struck him with His hand and treats him like a foe. Now, his friends render the same punishment through their words. Job wants to know when the unjust treatment will come to an end. He, however, is still assured that he will see the Father face to face. Although he believes the catastrophes are at the hand of God, he fails not in his hope of his eternal resting place with the heavenly Father.

Job was assured, that this Redeemer of sinners from the yoke of Satan and the condemnation of sin, was his Redeemer, and expected salvation through him; and that he was a living Redeemer, though not yet come in the flesh; and that at the last day he would appear as the Judge of the world, to raise the dead, and complete the redemption of his people. (Henry, 2014)

Let Job's faith serve as an example of one who stands on his beliefs regardless of what is occurring around him. When friends turn their back on you, when loved ones depart, when circumstances are unbearable, and when questions are left unanswered, God is yet in control of each and every situation. He may not answer when we think He should, but in due season, if we faint not, we shall hear from the Most High God.

If that is true, why hasn't God answered Job's queries yet? Just wait—He will!

This is a good opportunity to examine our own faith level. There are three main levels of faith, and different people are in different levels of faith in Jesus Christ (God).
There are people with
1. No faith (faithless)
2. Little faith (weak faith), and
3. Great faith (faithful)

Let us look at each one of these groups separately.

No faith (faithless)

These people have no faith in the Word, and they do not believe in Jesus Christ, but they have faith in other things which they believe in.

Saints, we should be careful with the faithless because they deny and pervert the truth bringing out controversies, miss-placed ideologies and doctrines. A good example of a faithless person is Thomas. Thomas was a disciple of Jesus, but when Jesus died, he became faithless. He did not believe that Jesus had risen from the dead as He had said.

> John: 20:27: *"Then he said to Thomas, Reach hither thy finger, and behold my hands; and reach hither thy hand, and thrust it into my side: and be not faithless, but believing."*

Realize that after Thomas saw resurrected Jesus Christ, he became of great faith and an apostle of the church.

With no faith you cannot believe in God. You doubt the Word of God, and you are always fighting the Word and God's children.

Little faith (weak faith)

People of little faith doubt everything. They doubt what they have heard, what they hear, the Word of God and they are always struggling to believe in God. With weak faith, you can neither experience the power of God nor have an intimacy with Him, and you doubt what the Spirit tells you.

A good example of a doubtful person in the Bible is Peter. Peter heard the word from Jesus to walk on the sea. He walked but upon seeing the wind, he started doubting and then sinking. Jesus said this to him, "........*O man of little faith, why did you doubt?"* (Matthew 14:31).

If you have weak faith or little faith, you are lukewarm, neither cold nor hot, a doubter, like the church at Laodicea. Doubters will never inherit the kingdom of heaven, for they are not of us: The Elect.

1 John 2:19 says, *"They went out from us, but they were not of us; for if they had been of us, they would no doubt have*

continued with us: but they went out, that they might be made manifest that they were not all of us."

Doubters according to the Word have no faith at all. Romans 14:23 says, *"And he that doubts is damned if he eat, because he eats not of faith: for whatsoever is not of faith is sin."* And because you are lukewarm, you will not inherit God's kingdom. Revelation 3:16 says, *"So, because you are lukewarm, and neither cold nor hot, I will spew you out of my mouth."*

People of little or weak faith are easily swayed away from the truth. When trials and temptations overcome them, they fall severally and continuously, always repenting and asking for forgiveness. If you doubt any of God's words, you are of little faith.

Examine yourself. In the three main levels of faith, where do you fall? Are you faithless or of little faith? Or, do you possess great faith? (Adapted from Christian Truth Center, 2015).

Those who have great faith trust God with their lives because they believe His Word. When a person has great faith, she does not doubt God, and she waits patiently for Him to move on her behalf.

The Bottom Line

Chapter Fifteen
The Wicked vs The Blessed

Chapter 20 Zophar

Then Zophar the Naamathite replied: ^{2} "My troubled thoughts prompt me to answer because I am greatly disturbed. ^{3} I hear a rebuke that dishonors me, and my understanding inspires me to reply. ^{4} "Surely you know how it has been from of old, ever since mankind was placed on the earth, ^{5} that the mirth of the wicked is brief, the joy of the godless lasts but a moment. ^{6} Though the pride of the godless person reaches to the heavens and his head touches the clouds, ^{7} he will perish forever, like his own dung; those who have seen him will say, 'Where is he?' ^{8} Like a dream he flies away, no more to be found, banished like a vision of the night. ^{9} The eye that saw him will not see him again; his place will look on him no more. ^{10} His children must make amends to the poor; his own hands must give back his wealth. ^{11} The youthful vigor that fills his bones will lie with him in the dust. ^{12} "Though evil is sweet in his mouth and he hides it under his tongue, ^{13} though he cannot bear to let it go and lets it linger in his mouth, ^{14} yet his food will turn sour in his stomach; it will become the venom of serpents within him. ^{15} He will spit out the riches he swallowed; God will make his stomach vomit them up. ^{16} He will suck the poison of serpents; the fangs of an adder will kill him. ⁱ⁷ He will not enjoy the streams, the rivers flowing with honey and cream. ¹⁸ What he toiled for he must give back uneaten; he will not enjoy the profit from his trading. ¹⁹ For he has oppressed the poor and left them destitute; he has seized houses he did not build. ²⁰ "Surely he will have no respite from his craving; he cannot save himself by his treasure. ²¹ Nothing is left for him to devour; his prosperity will not endure. ²² In the midst of his plenty, distress will overtake him; the full force of misery will come upon him. ²³ When he has filled his belly, God will vent his burning anger against him and rain down his blows on him. ²⁴ Though he flees from an iron weapon, a bronze-tipped arrow pierces him. ²⁵ He pulls it out of his back, the gleaming point out of his liver. Terrors will come over him; ²⁶ total darkness lies in wait for his treasures. A fire unfanned will consume him and devour what is left in his tent. ²⁷ The heavens will expose his guilt; the earth will rise up against him. ²⁸ A flood will carry off his house, rushing waters on the day of God's wrath. ²⁹ Such is the fate God allots the wicked, the heritage appointed for them by God."

Zophar is admittedly deeply troubled by the harsh words Job spoke towards them. Zophar feels dishonored and feels he needs to respond. He makes it clear that one who does evil and is puffed up in pride will suffer the wrath of God. If a wicked person has riches unspeakable, he will not be able to enjoy them for long. If he has peace of mind and restful nights, not fearing anything, it will not last. *"Distress will overtake him; the full force of misery will come upon him"* (v. 22).

In his lengthy retort, what Zophar does not make clear is whether he is directing his words directly at Job, or if he is telling Job that if he is indeed a wicked man as Job paints him to be, he will earn his just due as all wicked people will. In either case, the fate of the wicked is the same- the wrath of God.

Regardless of how man views us, God knows the truth, for He is omniscient. We can put on airs for people, we can live with false hope and peace, we can lie, steal and cheat to earn money, but in the end, we must give an account to God for the choices we have made. Sin begets wrath; while, honesty, love, and kindness beget blessings. And, as stated in Proverbs 10:22, *"The blessing of the LORD, it maketh rich, and he addeth no sorrow with it"* (KJV).

The Blessings of Christ, I Am Receiving!

Since the day I accepted Christ
and started believing…
Blessings from him,
I've been receiving!
Since the time I knelt down, and invited him in!
I have joy unspeakable! From deep within!
Since that day that I gave Christ an invitation.
I've been blessed with his mercy and salvation!
Since the time Christ came
and took my sins away…
He's given me hope and peace each day!
From the moment I allowed him to direct me…
His love and Holy Spirit have greatly touched me!
From this moment until the day
I'll see him face to face…

The Bottom Line

I'm going to keep receiving
his wonderful grace!
From this moment until the time
for my departure…
I'll meet him down here,
or meet him in the rapture!
From moment to moment,
with each passing year.
I'm going to love and keep
his word ever so near!
From this day on…
Won't you do the same!
And receive eternal life… In his name!
By Jim Pemberton

Chapter Sixteen
God is Just

Chapter 21 Job

Then Job replied: ² "Listen carefully to my words; let this be the consolation you give me. ³ Bear with me while I speak, and after I have spoken, mock on. ⁴ "Is my complaint directed to a human being? Why should I not be impatient? ⁵ Look at me and be appalled; clap your hand over your mouth. ⁶ When I think about this, I am terrified; trembling seizes my body. ⁷ Why do the wicked live on, growing old and increasing in power? ⁸ They see their children established around them, their offspring before their eyes. ⁹ Their homes are safe and free from fear; the rod of God is not on them. ¹⁰ Their bulls never fail to breed; their cows calve and do not miscarry. ¹¹ They send forth their children as a flock; their little ones dance about. ¹² They sing to the music of timbrel and lyre; they make merry to the sound of the pipe. ¹³ They spend their years in prosperity and go down to the grave in peace. ¹⁴ Yet they say to God, 'Leave us alone! We have no desire to know your ways. ¹⁵ Who is the Almighty, that we should serve him? What would we gain by praying to him?' ¹⁶ But their prosperity is not in their own hands, so I stand aloof from the plans of the wicked. ¹⁷ "Yet how often is the lamp of the wicked snuffed out? How often does calamity come upon them, the fate God allots in his

The Bottom Line

anger? [18] How often are they like straw before the wind, like chaff swept away by a gale? [19] It is said, 'God stores up the punishment of the wicked for their children.' Let him repay the wicked, so that they themselves will experience it! [20] Let their own eyes see their destruction; let them drink the cup of the wrath of the Almighty. [21] For what do they care about the families they leave behind when their allotted months come to an end? [22] "Can anyone teach knowledge to God, since he judges even the highest? [23] One person dies in full vigor, completely secure and at ease, [24] well nourished in body, bones rich with marrow. [25] Another dies in bitterness of soul, never having enjoyed anything good. [26] Side by side they lie in the dust, and worms cover them both. [27] "I know full well what you are thinking, the schemes by which you would wrong me. [28] You say, 'Where now is the house of the great, the tents where the wicked lived?' [29] Have you never questioned those who travel? Have you paid no regard to their accounts— [30] that the wicked are spared from the day of calamity, that they are delivered from the day of wrath? [31] Who denounces their conduct to their face? Who repays them for what they have done? [32] They are carried to the grave, and watch is kept over their tombs. [33] The soil in the valley is sweet to them; everyone follows after them, and a countless throng goes before them. [34] "So how can you console me with your nonsense? Nothing is left of your answers but falsehood!"

In this chapter, Job attempts to make the reasons for his impatience clear to his friends. They complain about the words he speaks to God, but Job begins by explaining God is not a mere mortal. Therefore, He can act at any given time, if He so chooses. From Job's perspective, the wicked are free to live lavishly with their families and their riches and even die in peace. The just, on the other hand, are left to suffer.

Job asks his friends to explain to him the justification of how things are and tells them they cannot console him with their nonsense. They insist the wicked will perish by God's rod, while the just live in peace. Job, from his own experiences, is not witnessing this reality for himself. His suffering is great.

Therefore, we can conclude what is readily apparent on the outside has nothing to with the content of one's heart. We must be careful about judging who is just and who is wicked and who deserves the wrath of God and who does not. When we attempt to do so, we may find ourselves in turmoil.

We are reminded in Isaiah 55:8, *"'For my thoughts are not your thoughts, neither are your ways my ways,' declares the LORD."* Matthew 7:1 says, *"Do not judge, or you too will be judged."* Therefore, we should leave judgment to God. *"God is just: He will pay back trouble to those who trouble you,"* says II Thessalonians 1:6.

The Bottom Line

Chapter Seventeen
Putting Others First

Chapter 22 Eliphaz

Then Eliphaz the Temanite replied: ² "Can a man be of benefit to God? Can even a wise person benefit him? ³ What pleasure would it give the Almighty if you were righteous? What would he gain if your ways were blameless? ⁴ "Is it for your piety that he rebukes you and brings charges against you? ⁵ Is not your wickedness great? Are not your sins endless? ⁶ You demanded security from your relatives for no reason; you stripped people of their clothing, leaving them naked. ⁷ You gave no water to the weary and you withheld food from the hungry, ⁸ though you were a powerful man, owning land— an honored man, living on it. ⁹ And you sent widows away empty-handed and broke the strength of the fatherless. ¹⁰ That is why snares are all around you, why sudden peril terrifies you, ¹¹ why it is so dark you cannot see, and why a flood of water covers you. ¹² "Is not God in the heights of heaven? And see how lofty are the highest stars! ¹³ Yet you say, 'What does God know? Does he judge through such darkness? ¹⁴ Thick clouds veil him, so he does not see us as he goes about in the vaulted heavens.' ¹⁵ Will you keep to the old path that the wicked have trod? ¹⁶ They were carried off before their time, their foundations washed away by a flood. ¹⁷ They said to God, 'Leave us alone! What can the

Almighty do to us?' ¹⁸ Yet it was he who filled their houses with good things, so I stand aloof from the plans of the wicked. ¹⁹ The righteous see their ruin and rejoice; the innocent mock them, saying, ²⁰ 'Surely our foes are destroyed, and fire devours their wealth.' ²¹ "Submit to God and be at peace with him; in this way prosperity will come to you. ²² Accept instruction from his mouth and lay up his words in your heart. ²³ If you return to the Almighty, you will be restored: If you remove wickedness far from your tent ²⁴ and assign your nuggets to the dust, your gold of Ophir to the rocks in the ravines, ²⁵ then the Almighty will be your gold, the choicest silver for you. ²⁶ Surely then you will find delight in the Almighty and will lift up your face to God. ²⁷ You will pray to him, and he will hear you, and you will fulfill your vows. ²⁸ What you decide on will be done, and light will shine on your ways. ²⁹ When people are brought low and you say, 'Lift them up!' then he will save the downcast. ³⁰ He will deliver even one who is not innocent, who will be delivered through the cleanness of your hands."

This time when Eliphaz speaks, he doesn't simply posit that Job is guilty of sin. He lists Job's supposed sins. The list includes demanding security from relatives without cause, failing to give water to the weary and food to the hungry, stripping people of their clothing, sending away widows empty-handed, and breaking the strength of the fatherless. Then, Eliphaz reminds Job that God sees all and judges all accordingly. Eliphaz admonishes Job to *"submit to God and be at peace with him; in this way prosperity will come to you"* (v. 21). He tells Job to remove wickedness from his heart and allow God to be everything for him. He declares if Job does those things, he will be able to lift his head up to God. Then, he could pray and God would hear him. Eliphaz insists Job will then be able to pray for others and God will grant his desires on their behalf because his heart and hands are clean.

What Eliphaz speaks of here is the power of intercessory prayer. When a person's heart is pure before God, she can pray on behalf of another, and God will hear her prayers. What is intercessory prayer?

Intercessory prayer is the act of praying for other people. The Lord instructed us to pray not only for our own personal needs but to reach out and pray for others as well. We find an example of this in 1 Timothy 2:1-6, where we are told to pray and to make intercession for all men. The Greek noun, "enteuxus" in the Bible is the word for "intercession." It primarily denotes a "meeting with," a conversation or petition rendered on the behalf of others. "Intercessory prayer," then, is seeking the presence and audience of God in another's stead. When we pray for the needs of others that is called "intercession" or we are said to be "interceding" for them. (Miller, 2013)

Scriptures on Intercessory Prayer

1 Timothy 2:1 ESV
First of all, then, I urge that supplications, prayers, intercessions, and thanksgivings be made for all people
Romans 8:26 ESV
Likewise the Spirit helps us in our weakness. For we do not know what to pray for as we ought, but the Spirit himself intercedes for us with groanings too deep for words.

Matthew 18:19-20 ESV

Again I say to you, if two of you agree on earth about anything they ask, it will be done for them by my Father in heaven. For where two or three are gathered in my name, there am I among them."

James 5:13-16 ESV

Is anyone among you suffering? Let him pray. Is anyone cheerful? Let him sing praise. Is anyone among you sick? Let him call for the elders of the church, and let them pray over him, anointing him with oil in the name of the Lord. And the prayer of faith will save the one who is sick, and the Lord will raise him up. And if he has committed sins, he will be forgiven. Therefore, confess your sins to one another and pray for one another, that you may be healed. The prayer of a righteous person has great power as it is working.

Ephesians 6:18 ESV

Praying at all times in the Spirit, with all prayer and supplication. To that end keep alert with all perseverance, making supplication for all the saints

Isaiah 59:16 (ESV)

He saw that there was no man, and wondered that there was no one to intercede; then his own arm brought him salvation, and his righteousness upheld him.

2 Corinthians 1:11

You also joining in helping us through your prayers, so that thanks may be given by many persons on our behalf for the favor bestowed on us through the prayers of many.

Chapter Eighteen
Suffering for the Righteous

Chapter 23 Job

Then Job replied: ² "Even today my complaint is bitter; his hand is heavy in spite of my groaning. ³ If only I knew where to find him; if only I could go to his dwelling! ⁴ I would state my case before him and fill my mouth with arguments. ⁵ I would find out what he would answer me, and consider what he would say to me. ⁶ Would he vigorously oppose me? No, he would not press charges against me. ⁷ There the upright can establish their innocence before him, and there I would be delivered forever from my judge. ⁸ "But if I go to the east, he is not there; if I go to the west, I do not find him. ⁹ When he is at work in the north, I do not see him; when he turns to the south, I catch no glimpse of him. ¹⁰ But he knows the way that I take; when he has tested me, I will come forth as gold. ¹¹ My feet have closely followed his steps; I have kept to his way without turning aside. ¹² I have not departed from the commands of his lips; I have treasured the words of his mouth more than my daily bread. ¹³ "But he stands alone, and who can oppose him? He does whatever he pleases. ¹⁴ He carries out his decree against me, and many such plans he still has in store. ¹⁵ That is why I am terrified before him; when I think of all this, I fear him. ¹⁶ God has made my heart faint; the

Almighty has terrified me. [17] Yet I am not silenced by the darkness, by the thick darkness that covers my face.

Chapter 24 Job Continues

"Why does the Almighty not set times for judgment? Why must those who know him look in vain for such days? [2] There are those who move boundary stones; they pasture flocks they have stolen. [3] They drive away the orphan's donkey and take the widow's ox in pledge. [4] They thrust the needy from the path and force all the poor of the land into hiding. [5] Like wild donkeys in the desert, the poor go about their labor of foraging food; the wasteland provides food for their children. [6] They gather fodder in the fields and glean in the vineyards of the wicked. [7] Lacking clothes, they spend the night naked; they have nothing to cover themselves in the cold. [8] They are drenched by mountain rains and hug the rocks for lack of shelter. [9] The fatherless child is snatched from the breast; the infant of the poor is seized for a debt. [10] Lacking clothes, they go about naked; they carry the sheaves, but still go hungry. [11] They crush olives among the terraces; they tread the winepresses, yet suffer thirst. [12] The groans of the dying rise from the city, and the souls of the wounded cry out for help. But God charges no one with wrongdoing. [13] "There are those who rebel against the light, who do not know its ways or stay in its paths. [14] When daylight is gone, the murderer rises up, kills the poor and needy, and in the night steals forth like a thief. [15] The eye of the adulterer watches for dusk; he thinks, 'No eye will see me,' and he keeps his face concealed. [16] In the dark, thieves break into houses, but by day they shut themselves in; they want nothing to do with the light. [17] For all of them, midnight is their *morning; they make friends with the terrors of darkness.* [18] *"Yet they are foam on the surface of the water; their portion of the land is cursed, so that no one goes to the vineyards.* [19] *As heat and drought snatch away the melted snow, so the grave snatches away those who have sinned.* [20] *The womb forgets them, the worm feasts on them; the wicked are no longer remembered but are broken like a tree.* [21] *They prey on the barren and childless woman, and to the widow they show no kindness.* [22] *But God drags away the mighty by his power; though they become established, they have no assurance of life.* [23] *He may let them rest in a feeling of security, but his eyes are on their ways.* [24] *For a little while they are exalted, and then they are gone; they are brought low and gathered up like all others; they are cut off like heads of grain.* [25] *"If this is not so, who can prove me false and reduce my words to nothing?"*

Job says if he could go to God's throne and state his case, God would not deny him for he is not guilty. He proclaims he has followed the way of the Lord and heeded his commands. He continues in his belief that his calamity is at the hand of God and admits his fear of God. He goes on to provide extensive examples of the wicked who seemingly suffer no wrath. But the eyes of God are on them, and eventually, they will pay a hefty price. They rest in false security, but in the end, their rest and peace is snatched away.

What point is Job attempting to make? Don't his friends think he fits that very profile? Job's life was contrary to those examples and his friends admitted as much when they stated he had counseled others. Job had gone about doing good. He even offered burnt offerings to God when he believed his children sinned against God. Job was conscious of righteous living- not only in his life but in those of his children.

Chapter Nineteen
God's Sovereignty

Chapter 25 Bildad Speaks
Then Bildad the Shuhite replied: [2] "Dominion and awe belong to God; he establishes order in the heights of heaven. [3] Can his forces be numbered? On whom does his light not rise? [4] How then can a mortal be righteous before God? How can one born of woman be pure? [5] If even the moon is not bright and the stars are not pure in his eyes, [6] how much less a mortal, who is but a maggot— a human being, who is only a worm!"

Bildad offers a descriptive contrast between God and man. God has dominion over the universe, while man has no power, except that which God gives him. God is to be revered for His holiness, His righteousness, His justice, His awesomeness, and His majesty, while man is clothed in flesh, which has no good thing in it. Man is only viewed as righteous once he has accepted Christ as his Lord and Saviour and Christ's righteousness is imputed unto him. Also, God establishes order in the heavens, while man remains disorderly on Earth. Plain and simple, man is in no way comparable to God.

"Sin is cosmic treason. Sin is treason against a perfectly pure Sovereign. It is an act of supreme ingratitude toward the One to whom we owe everything, to the One who has given us life itself. Have you ever considered the deeper implications of the slightest sin, of the most minute peccadillo? What are we saying to our Creator when we disobey Him at the slightest point? We are saying no to the righteousness of God. We are saying, "God, Your law is not good. My judgement is better than Yours. Your authority does not apply to me. I am above and beyond Your jurisdiction. I have the right to do what I want to do, not what You command me to do."

— R.C. Sproul, *The Holiness of God*

Chapter Twenty
Declaration of Innocence

Chapter 26 Final Word to His Friends

Then Job replied: ² "How you have helped the powerless! How you have saved the arm that is feeble! ³ What advice you have offered to one without wisdom! And what great insight you hav displayed! ⁴ Who has helped you utter these words? And whose spirit spoke from your mouth? ⁵ "The dead are in deep anguish, those beneath the waters and all that live in them. ⁶ The realm of the dead is naked before God; Destruction lies uncovered. ⁷ He spreads out the northern skies over empty space; he suspends the earth over nothing. ⁸ He wraps up the waters in his clouds, yet the clouds do not burst under their weight. ⁹ He covers the face of the full moon, spreading his clouds over it. ¹⁰ He marks out the horizon on the face of the waters for a boundary between light and darkness. ¹¹ The pillars of the heavens quake, aghast at his rebuke. ¹² By his power he churned up the sea; by his wisdom he cut Rahab to pieces. ¹³ By his breath the skies became fair; his hand pierced the gliding serpent. ¹⁴ And these are but the outer fringe of his works; how faint the whisper we hear of him! Who then can understand the thunder of his power?"

Chapter 27 Job Continues

And Job continued his discourse: *² "As surely as God lives, who has denied me justice, the Almighty, who has made my life bitter, ³ as long as I have life within me, the breath of God in my nostrils, ⁴ my lips will not say anything wicked, and my tongue will not utter lies. ⁵ I will never admit you are in the right; till I die, I will not deny my integrity. ⁶ I will maintain my innocence and never let go of it; my conscience will not reproach me as long as I live. ⁷ "May my enemy be like the wicked, my adversary like the unjust! ⁸ For what hope have the godless when they are cut off, when God takes away their life? ⁹ Does God listen to their cry when distress comes upon them? ¹⁰ Will they find delight in the Almighty? Will they call on God at all times? ¹¹ "I will teach you about the power of God; the ways of the Almighty I will not conceal. ¹² You have all seen this yourselves. Why then this meaningless talk? ¹³ "Here is the fate God allots to the wicked, the heritage a ruthless man receives from the Almighty: ¹⁴ However many his children, their fate is the sword; his offspring will never have enough to eat. ¹⁵ The plague will bury those who survive him, and their widows will not weep for them. ¹⁶ Though he heaps up silver like dust and clothes like piles of clay, ¹⁷ what he lays up the righteous will wear, and the innocent will divide his silver. ¹⁸ The house he builds is like a moth's cocoon, like a hut made by a watchman. ¹⁹ He lies down wealthy, but will do so no more; when he opens his eyes, all is gone. ²⁰ Terrors overtake him like a flood; a tempest snatches him away in the night. ²¹ The east wind carries him off, and he is gone; it sweeps him out of his place. ²² It hurls itself against him without mercy as he flees headlong from its power. ²³ It claps its hands in derision and hisses him out of his place."*

In these two chapters, Job begins what is his final response to his friends- declaring his innocence. His complete response occurs in Chapters 26-27 and 29-31. Chapter 28 is an interlude to wisdom.

Job questions his friends about which spirit controls their tongues and causes them to utter the words they say. He goes on to describe the mighty powers of God. Job stands his ground and his innocence while he continues to educate his friends on the ways of God. First, he discusses the imminent destruction of the wicked: all he has will perish and come to naught.

Job's friends, on the same subject, spoke of the misery of wicked men before death as proportioned to their crimes; Job considered that if it were not so, still the consequences of their death would be dreadful. Job undertook to set this matter in a true light. Death to a godly man, is like a fair gale of wind to convey him to the heavenly country; but, to a wicked man, it is like a storm, that hurries him away to destruction.

While he lived, he had the benefit of sparing mercy; but now the day of God's patience is over, and he will pour out upon him his wrath. When God casts down a man, there is no flying from, nor bearing up under his anger. Those who will not now flee to the arms of Divine grace, which are stretched out to receive them, will not be able to flee from the arms of Divine wrath, which will shortly be stretched out to destroy them. And what is a man profited if he gain the whole world, and thus lose his own soul? (Matthew Henry's Concise Commentary)

James 3:8 says, *"But no human being can tame the tongue. It is a restless evil, full of deadly poison."*

Chapter Twenty-One
Curiosity

Chapter 28 Interlude: Where Wisdom Is Found

There is a mine for silver and a place where gold is refined. ^{2} Iron is taken from the earth, and copper is smelted from ore. ^{3} Mortals put an end to the darkness; they search out the farthest recesses for ore in the blackest darkness. ^{4} Far from human dwellings they cut a shaft, in places untouched by human feet; far from other people they dangle and sway. ^{5} The earth, from which food comes, is transformed below as by fire; ^{6} lapis lazuli comes from its rocks, and its dust contains nuggets of gold. ^{7} No bird of prey knows that hidden path, no falcon's eye has seen it. ^{8} Proud beasts do not set foot on it, and no lion prowls there. ^{9} People assault the flinty rock with their hands and lay bare the roots of the mountains. ^{10} They tunnel through the rock; their eyes see all its treasures. ^{11} They search the sources of the rivers and bring hidden things to light. ^{12} But where can wisdom be found? Where does understanding dwell? ^{13} No mortal comprehends its worth; it cannot be found in the land of the living. ^{14} The deep says, "It is not in me"; the sea says, "It is not with me." ^{15} It cannot be bought with the finest gold, nor can its price be weighed out in silver. ^{16} It cannot be bought with the gold of Ophir, with precious onyx or lapis lazuli. ^{17} Neither gold nor crystal can *compare with it, nor can it be had for jewels of gold. ¹⁸ Coral and jasper are not worthy of mention; the price of wisdom is beyond rubies. ¹⁹ The topaz of Cush cannot compare with it; it cannot be bought with pure gold. ²⁰ Where then does wisdom come from? Where does understanding dwell? ²¹ It is hidden from the eyes of every living thing, concealed even from the birds in the sky. ²² Destruction and Death say, "Only a rumor of it has reached our ears." ²³ God understands the way to it and he alone knows where it dwells, ²⁴ for he views the ends of the earth and sees everything under the heavens. ²⁵ When he established the force of the wind and measured out the waters, ²⁶ when he made a decree for the rain and a path for the thunderstorm, ²⁷ then he looked at wisdom and appraised it; he confirmed it and tested it. ²⁸ And he said to the human race, "The fear of the Lord—that is wisdom, and to shun evil is understanding."*

Humans are described in this passage to always be seeking the unknown by tapping into uncharted waters and undiscovered land. Humans will endeavor to go where other creatures refrain from going. What man should seek after is wisdom. Wisdom is not something that can be purchased- for any cost. It must be obtained from God. One demonstrates her wisdom by fearing the Lord, revering him.

The Bible says in James 1:5 *"If any of you lack wisdom, let him ask of God, that giveth to all men liberally, and upbraideth not; and it shall be given him."*

Chapter Twenty-Two
One Final Thought

Chapter 29 Job's Final Defense Continued

Job continued his discourse: ² "How I long for the months gone by, for the days when God watched over me, ³ when his lamp shone on my head and by his light I walked through darkness! ⁴ Oh, for the days when I was in my prime, when God's intimate friendship blessed my house, ⁵ when the Almighty was still with me and my children were around me, ⁶ when my path was drenched with cream and the rock poured out for me streams of olive oil. ⁷ "When I went to the gate of the city and took my seat in the public square, ⁸ the young men saw me and stepped aside and the old men rose to their feet; ⁹ the chief men refrained from speaking and covered their mouths with their hands; ¹⁰ the voices of the nobles were hushed, and their tongues stuck to the roof of their mouths. ¹¹ Whoever heard me spoke well of me, and those who saw me commended me, ¹² because I rescued the poor who cried for help, and the fatherless who had none to assist them. ¹³ The one who was dying blessed me; I made the widow's heart sing. ¹⁴ I put on righteousness as my clothing; justice was my robe and my turban. ¹⁵ I was eyes to the blind and feet to the lame.¹⁶ I was a father to the needy; I took up the case of the stranger. ¹⁷ I broke the fangs of the wicked and snatched the victims from their teeth. [18] "I thought, 'I will die in my own house, my days as numerous as the grains of sand. [19] My roots will reach to the water, and the dew will lie all night on my branches. [20] My glory will not fade; the bow will be ever new in my hand.' [21] "People listened to me expectantly, waiting in silence for my counsel. [22] After I had spoken, they spoke no more; my words fell gently on their ears. [23] They waited for me as for showers and drank in my words as the spring rain. [24] When I smiled at them, they scarcely believed it; the light of my face was precious to them [25] I chose the way for them and sat as their chief; I dwelt as a king among his troops; I was like one who comforts mourners.

Chapter 30 Continued

"But now they mock me, men younger than I, whose fathers I would have disdained to put with my sheep dogs. [2] Of what use was the strength of their hands to me, since their vigor had gone from them? [3] Haggard from want and hunger, they roamed the parched land in desolate wastelands at night. [4] In the brush they gathered salt herbs, and their food was the root of the broom bush. [5] They were banished from human society, shouted at as if they were thieves. [6] They were forced to live in the dry stream beds, among the rocks and in holes in the ground. [7] They brayed among the bushes and huddled in the undergrowth. [8] A base and nameless brood, they were driven out of the land. [9] "And now those young men mock me in song; I have become a byword among them. [10] They detest me and keep their distance; they do not hesitate to spit in my face. [11] Now that God has unstrung my bow and afflicted me, they throw off restraint in my presence. [12] On my right the tribe attacks; they lay snares for my feet, they build their siege ramps against me. ⁱ³ They break up my road; they succeed in destroying me. 'No one can help him,' they say. ¹⁴ They advance as through a gaping breach; amid the ruins they come rolling in. ¹⁵ Terrors overwhelm me; my dignity is driven away as by the wind, my safety vanishes like a cloud. ¹⁶ "And now my life ebbs away; days of suffering grip me. ¹⁷ Night pierces my bones; my gnawing pains never rest. ¹⁸ In his great power God becomes like clothing to me; he binds me like the neck of my garment. ¹⁹ He throws me into the mud, and I am reduced to dust and ashes. ²⁰ "I cry out to you, God, but you do not answer; I stand up, but you merely look at me. ²¹ You turn on me ruthlessly; with the might of your hand you attack me. ²² You snatch me up and drive me before the wind; you toss me about in the storm. ²³ I know you will bring me down to death, to the place appointed for all the living. ²⁴ "Surely no one lays a hand on a broken man when he cries for help in his distress. ²⁵ Have I not wept for those in trouble? Has not my soul grieved for the poor? ²⁶ Yet when I hoped for good, evil came; when I looked for light, then came darkness. ²⁷ The churning inside me never stops; days of suffering confront me. ²⁸ I go about blackened, but not by the sun; I stand up in the assembly and cry for help. ²⁹ I have become a brother of jackals, a companion of owls. ³⁰ My skin grows black and peels; my body burns with fever. ³¹ My lyre is tuned to mourning, and my pipe to the sound of wailing.

Chapter 31 Continued

"I made a covenant with my eyes not to look lustfully at a young woman. ² For what is our lot from God above, our heritage from the Almighty on high? ³ Is it not ruin for the wicked, disaster for those who do wrong? ⁴ Does he not see my ways and count my every step? ⁵ "If I have walked with falsehood or my foot has hurried after deceit— ⁶ let God weigh me in honest scales and he will know that I am blameless— ⁷ if my steps have turned from the path, if my heart has been led by my eyes, or if my hands have been defiled, ⁸ then may others eat what I have sown, and may my crops be uprooted. ⁹ "If my heart has been enticed by a woman, or if I have lurked at my neighbor's door, ¹⁰ then may my wife grind another man's grain, and may other men sleep with her. ¹¹ For that would have been wicked, a sin to be judged. ¹² It is a fire that burns to Destruction; it would have uprooted my harvest. ¹³ "If I have denied justice to any of my servants, whether male or female, when they had a grievance against me, ¹⁴ what will I do when God confronts me? What will I answer when called to account? ¹⁵ Did not he who made me in the womb make them? Did not the same one form us both within our mothers? ¹⁶ "If I have denied the desires of the poor or let the eyes of the widow grow weary, ¹⁷ if I have kept my bread to myself, not sharing it with the fatherless— ¹⁸ but from my youth I reared them as a father would, and from my birth I guided the widow— ¹⁹ if I have seen anyone perishing for lack of clothing, or the needy without garments, ²⁰ and their hearts did not bless me for warming them with the fleece from my sheep, ²¹ if I have raised my hand against the fatherless, knowing that I had influence in court, ²² then let my arm fall from the shoulder, let it be broken off at the joint. ²³ For I dreaded destruction from God, and for fear of his splendor I could not do such things. ²⁴ "If I have put my trust in gold or said to pure *gold, 'You are my security,'* ²⁵ *if I have rejoiced over my great wealth, the fortune my hands had gained,* ²⁶ *if I have regarded the sun in its radiance or the moon moving in splendor,* ²⁷ *so that my heart was secretly enticed and my hand offered them a kiss of homage,* ²⁸ *then these also would be sins to be judged, for I would have been unfaithful to God on high.* ²⁹ *"If I have rejoiced at my enemy's misfortune or gloated over the trouble that came to him—* ³⁰ *I have not allowed my mouth to sin by invoking a curse against their life—*³¹ *if those of my household have never said, 'Who has not been filled with Job's meat?'—*³² *but no stranger had to spend the night in the street, for my door was always open to the traveler—* ³³ *if I have concealed my sin as people do, by hiding my guilt in my heart* ³⁴ *because I so feared the crowd and so dreaded the contempt of the clans that I kept silent and would not go outside—* ³⁵ *("Oh, that I had someone to hear me! I sign now my defense—let the Almighty answer me; let my accuser put his indictment in writing.* ³⁶ *Surely I would wear it on my shoulder, I would put it on like a crown.* ³⁷ *I would give him an account of my every step; I would present it to him as to a ruler.)—* ³⁸ *"if my land cries out against me and all its furrows are wet with tears,* ³⁹ *if I have devoured its yield without payment or broken the spirit of its tenants,* ⁴⁰ *then let briers come up instead of wheat and stinkweed instead of barley." The words of Job are ended.*

Job's friends' biggest complaint against Job was hypocrisy. Their claim was Job professed to be honorable and upright before God. He claimed to love God. But, they maintain if Job loved God, he would not be facing the destruction he was presently facing. They provided example after example each time they spoke.

Job proceeds to contrast his former prosperity with his present misery, through God's withdrawing from him. A gracious soul delights in God's smiles, not in the smiles of this world. Four things were then very pleasant to holy Job. 1. The confidence he had in the Divine protection. 2. The enjoyment he had of the Divine favour. 3. The communion he had with the Divine word. 4. The assurance he had of the Divine presence. God's presence with a man in his house, though it be but a cottage, makes it a castle and a palace. Then also he had comfort in his family.

Riches and flourishing families, like a candle, may be soon extinguished. But when the mind is enlightened by the Holy Spirit, when a man walks in the light of God's countenance, every outward comfort is doubled, every trouble is diminished, and he may pass cheerfully by this light through life and through death. Yet the sensible comfort of this state is often withdrawn for a season; and commonly this arises from sinful neglect, and grieving the Holy Spirit: sometimes it may be a trial of a man's faith and grace. But it is needful to examine ourselves, to seek for the cause of such a change by fervent prayer, and to increase our watchfulness.

All sorts of people paid respect to Job, not only for the dignity of his rank, but for his personal merit, his prudence, integrity, and good management. Happy the men who are blessed with such gifts as these! They have great opportunities of honouring God and doing good, but have great need to watch against pride. Happy the people who are blessed with such men! It is a token for good to them.

Here we see what Job valued himself by, in the day of his prosperity. It was by his usefulness. He valued himself by the check he gave to the violence of proud and evil men. Good magistrates must thus be a restraint to evil-doers, and protect the innocent; in order to this, they should arm themselves with zeal and resolution. Such men are public blessings, and resemble Him who rescues poor sinners from Satan. How many who were ready to perish, now are blessing Him! But who can show forth His praises? May we trust in His mercy, and seek to imitate His truth, justice, and love. (Henry, 2014)

The Bottom Line

Chapter Twenty-Three
An Interjection

Chapter 32 Elihu

So these three men stopped answering Job, because he was righteous in his own eyes. ² But Elihu son of Barakel the Buzite, of the family of Ram, became very angry with Job for justifying himself rather than God. ³ He was also angry with the three friends, because they had found no way to refute Job, and yet had condemned him. ⁴ Now Elihu had waited before speaking to Job because they were older than he. ⁵ But when he saw that the three men had nothing more to say, his anger was aroused. ⁶ So Elihu son of Barakel the Buzite said: "I am young in years, and you are old; that is why I was fearful, not daring to tell you what I know. ⁷ I thought, 'Age should speak; advanced years should teach wisdom.' ⁸ But it is the spirit in a person, the breath of the Almighty, that gives them understanding. ⁹ It is not only the old who are wise, not only the aged who understand what is right. ¹⁰ "Therefore I say: Listen to me; I too will tell you what I know. ¹¹ I waited while you spoke, I listened to your reasoning; while you were searching for words, ¹² I gave you my full attention. But not one of you has proved Job wrong; none of you has answered his arguments. ¹³ Do not say, 'We have found wisdom; let God, not a man, refute him.' ¹⁴ But Job has not marshaled his words against me, and I will not answer him with your arguments. ^{15} "They are dismayed and have no more to say; words have failed them. ^{16} Must I wait, now that they are silent, now that they stand there with no reply? ^{17} I too will have my say; I too will tell what I know. ^{18} For I am full of words, and the spirit within me compels me; ^{19} inside I am like bottled-up wine, like new wineskins ready to burst. ^{20} I must speak and find relief; I must open my lips and reply. ^{21} I will show no partiality, nor will I flatter anyone; ^{22} for if I were skilled in flattery, my Maker would soon take me away.

Chapter 33 Elihu Continues

"But now, Job, listen to my words; pay attention to everything I say. ^{2} I am about to open my mouth; my words are on the tip of my tongue. ^{3} My words come from an upright heart; my lips sincerely speak what I know. ^{4} The Spirit of God has made me; the breath of the Almighty gives me life. ^{5} Answer me then, if you can; stand up and argue your case before me. ^{6} I am the same as you in God's sight; I too am a piece of clay. ^{7} No fear of me should alarm you, nor should my hand be heavy on you. ^{8} "But you have said in my hearing— I heard the very words— ^{9} 'I am pure, I have done no wrong; I am clean and free from sin. ^{10} Yet God has found fault with me; he considers me his enemy. ^{11} He fastens my feet in shackles; he keeps close watch on all my paths.' ^{12} "But I tell you, in this you are not right, for God is greater than any mortal. ^{13} Why do you complain to him that he responds to no one's words? ^{14} For God does speak—now one way, now another— though no one perceives it. ^{15} In a dream, in a vision of the night, when deep sleep falls on people as they slumber in their beds, ^{16} he may speak in their ears and terrify them with warnings, [17] to turn them from wrongdoing and keep them from pride, [18] to preserve them from the pit, their lives from perishing by the sword. [19] "Or someone may be chastened on a bed of pain with constant distress in their bones, [20] so that their body finds food repulsive and their soul loathes the choicest meal. [21] Their flesh wastes away to nothing, and their bones, once hidden, now stick out. [22] They draw near to the pit, and their life to the messengers of death. [23] Yet if there is an angel at their side, a messenger, one out of a thousand, sent to tell them how to be upright, [24] and he is gracious to that person and says to God, 'Spare them from going down to the pit; I have found a ransom for them— [25] let their flesh be renewed like a child's; let them be restored as in the days of their youth'— [26] then that person can pray to God and find favor with him, they will see God's face and shout for joy; he will restore them to full well-being. [27] And they will go to others and say, 'I have sinned, I have perverted what is right, but I did not get what I deserved. [28] God has delivered me from going down to the pit, and I shall live to enjoy the light of life.' [29] "God does all these things to a person— twice, even three times— [30] to turn them back from the pit, that the light of life may shine on them. [31] "Pay attention, Job, and listen to me; be silent, and I will speak. [32] If you have anything to say, answer me; speak up, for I want to vindicate you. [33] But if not, then listen to me; be silent, and I will teach you wisdom."

Chapter 34 Elihu Continues

Then Elihu said: [2] "Hear my words, you wise men; listen to me, you men of learning. [3] For the ear tests words as the tongue tastes food. [4] Let us discern for ourselves what is right; let us *learn together what is good. ⁵ "Job says, 'I am innocent, but God denies me justice. ⁶ Although I am right, I am considered a liar; although I am guiltless, his arrow inflicts an incurable wound.' ⁷ Is there anyone like Job, who drinks scorn like water? ⁸ He keeps company with evildoers; he associates with the wicked. ⁹ For he says, 'There is no profit in trying to please God.' ¹⁰ "So listen to me, you men of understanding. Far be it from God to do evil, from the Almighty to do wrong. ¹¹ He repays everyone for what they have done; he brings on them what their conduct deserves. ¹² It is unthinkable that God would do wrong, that the Almighty would pervert justice. ¹³ Who appointed him over the earth? Who put him in charge of the whole world? ¹⁴ If it were his intention and he withdrew his spirit and breath, ¹⁵ all humanity would perish together and mankind would return to the dust. ¹⁶ "If you have understanding, hear this; listen to what I say. ¹⁷ Can someone who hates justice govern? Will you condemn the just and mighty One? ¹⁸ Is he not the One who says to kings, 'You are worthless,' and to nobles, 'You are wicked,' ¹⁹ who shows no partiality to princes and does not favor the rich over the poor, for they are all the work of his hands? ²⁰ They die in an instant, in the middle of the night; the people are shaken and they pass away; the mighty are removed without human hand. ²¹ "His eyes are on the ways of mortals; he sees their every step. ²² There is no deep shadow, no utter darkness, where evildoers can hide. ²³ God has no need to examine people further, that they should come before him for judgment. ²⁴ Without inquiry he shatters the mighty and sets up others in their place. ²⁵ Because he takes note of their deeds, he overthrows them in the night and they are crushed. ²⁶ He* punishes them for their wickedness where everyone can see them, [27] because they turned from following him and had no regard for any of his ways. [28] They caused the cry of the poor to come before him, so that he heard the cry of the needy. [29] But if he remains silent, who can condemn him? If he hides his face, who can see him? Yet he is over individual and nation alike, [30] to keep the godless from ruling, from laying snares for the people. [31] "Suppose someone says to God, 'I am guilty but will offend no more. [32] Teach me what I cannot see; if I have done wrong, I will not do so again.' [33] Should God then reward you on your terms, when you refuse to repent? You must decide, not I; so tell me what you know. [34] "Men of understanding declare, wise men who hear me say to me, [35] 'Job speaks without knowledge; his words lack insight.' [36] Oh, that Job might be tested to the utmost for answering like a wicked man! [37] To his sin he adds rebellion; scornfully he claps his hands among us and multiplies his words against God."

Chapter 35 Elihu Continues

Then Elihu said: [2] "Do you think this is just? You say, 'I am in the right, not God.' [3] Yet you ask him, 'What profit is it to me, and what do I gain by not sinning?' [4] "I would like to reply to you and to your friends with you. [5] Look up at the heavens and see; gaze at the clouds so high above you. [6] If you sin, how does that affect him? If your sins are many, what does that do to him? [7] If you are righteous, what do you give to him, or what does he receive from your hand? [8] Your wickedness only affects humans like yourself, and your righteousness only other people. [9] "People cry out under a load of oppression; they plead for relief from the arm of the powerful. [10] But no one says, 'Where is God my Maker, who gives songs in the night, ¹¹ who teaches us more than he teaches the beasts of the earth and makes us wiser than the birds in the sky?' ¹² He does not answer when people cry out because of the arrogance of the wicked. ¹³ Indeed, God does not listen to their empty plea; the Almighty pays no attention to it. ¹⁴ How much less, then, will he listen when you say that you do not see him, that your case is before him and you must wait for him, ¹⁵ and further, that his anger never punishes and he does not take the least notice of wickedness. ¹⁶ So Job opens his mouth with empty talk; without knowledge he multiplies words."

Chapter 36 Elihu Continues

Elihu continued: ² "Bear with me a little longer and I will show you that there is more to be said in God's behalf. ³ I get my knowledge from afar; I will ascribe justice to my Maker. ⁴ Be assured that my words are not false; one who has perfect knowledge is with you. ⁵ "God is mighty, but despises no one; he is mighty, and firm in his purpose. ⁶ He does not keep the wicked alive but gives the afflicted their rights. ⁷ He does not take his eyes off the righteous; he enthrones them with kings and exalts them forever. ⁸ But if people are bound in chains, held fast by cords of affliction, ⁹ he tells them what they have done—that they have sinned arrogantly. ¹⁰ He makes them listen to correction and commands them to repent of their evil. ¹¹ If they obey and serve him, they will spend the rest of their days in prosperity and their years in contentment. ¹² But if they do not listen, they will perish by the sword and die without knowledge. ¹³ "The godless in heart harbor resentment; even when he fetters them, they do not cry for help. ¹⁴ They die in *their youth, among male prostitutes of the shrines. ¹⁵ But those who suffer he delivers in their suffering; he speaks to them in their affliction. ¹⁶ "He is wooing you from the jaws of distress to a spacious place free from restriction, to the comfort of your table laden with choice food. ¹⁷ But now you are laden with the judgment due the wicked; judgment and justice have taken hold of you. ¹⁸ Be careful that no one entices you by riches; do not let a large bribe turn you aside. ¹⁹ Would your wealth or even all your mighty efforts sustain you so you would not be in distress? ²⁰ Do not long for the night, to drag people away from their homes. ²¹ Beware of turning to evil, which you seem to prefer to affliction. ²² "God is exalted in his power. Who is a teacher like him? ²³ Who has prescribed his ways for him, or said to him, 'You have done wrong'? ²⁴ Remember to extol his work, which people have praised in song. ²⁵ All humanity has seen it; mortals gaze on it from afar. ²⁶ How great is God—beyond our understanding! The number of his years is past finding out. ²⁷ "He draws up the drops of water, which distill as rain to the streams; ²⁸ the clouds pour down their moisture and abundant showers fall on mankind. ²⁹ Who can understand how he spreads out the clouds, how he thunders from his pavilion? ³⁰ See how he scatters his lightning about him, bathing the depths of the sea. ³¹ This is the way he governs the nations and provides food in abundance. ³² He fills his hands with lightning and commands it to strike its mark. ³³ His thunder announces the coming storm; even the cattle make known its approach.*

Chapter 37 Elihu Continues

"At this my heart pounds and leaps from its place. ² Listen! Listen to the roar of his voice, to the rumbling that comes from his mouth. ³ He unleashes his lightning beneath the whole heaven and sends it to the ends of the earth. ⁴ After that comes the sound of his roar; he thunders with his majestic voice. When his voice resounds, he holds nothing back. ⁵ God's voice thunders in marvelous ways; he does great things beyond our understanding. ⁶ He says to the snow, 'Fall on the earth,' and to the rain shower, 'Be a mighty downpour.' ⁷ So that everyone he has made may know his work, he stops all people from their labor. ⁸ The animals take cover; they remain in their dens. ⁹ The tempest comes out from its chamber, the cold from the driving winds. ¹⁰ The breath of God produces ice, and the broad waters become frozen. ¹¹ He loads the clouds with moisture; he scatters his lightning through them. ¹² At his direction they swirl around over the face of the whole earth to do whatever he commands them. ¹³ He brings the clouds to punish people, or to water his earth and show his love. ¹⁴ "Listen to this, Job; stop and consider God's wonders. ¹⁵ Do you know how God controls the clouds and makes his lightning flash? ¹⁶ Do you know how the clouds hang poised, those wonders of him who has perfect knowledge? ¹⁷ You who swelter in your clothes when the land lies hushed under the south wind, ¹⁸ can you join him in spreading out the skies, hard as a mirror of cast bronze? ¹⁹ "Tell us what we should say to him; we cannot draw up our case because of our darkness. ²⁰ Should he be told that I want to speak? Would anyone ask to be swallowed up? ²¹ Now no one can look at the sun, bright as it is in the skies after the wind has swept them clean. ²² Out of the *north he comes in golden splendor; God comes in awesome majesty. ²³ The Almighty is beyond our reach and exalted in power; in his justice and great righteousness, he does not oppress. ²⁴ Therefore, people revere him, for does he not have regard for all the wise in heart?*

From Chapter 3 to Chapter 31, Job and his three friends engage in a heated debate, where each side tries to prove its perspective to the other side. Job, on one side, declares his innocence and shows the harshness of God, although He believes God is just. Eliphaz, Bildad, and Zophar, on the other side, declare Job's guilt and attempt to prove it by way of examples. In the end, there is much circular conversation and not one of them convinces the other of side.

After Job's final elocution, his friends do not respond any further. They decide *"he is righteous in his own eyes"* (v. 1). Proverbs 3:5-6 states, *"Trust in the LORD with all thine heart; and lean not unto thine own understanding. In all thy ways acknowledge him, and he shall direct thy paths."* Therefore, we would be wise to trust God in His infinite wisdom in all matters.

In Chapter 32,
> a young man appears on the scene named Elihu. His speech goes all the way through Chapter 37. Here, we learn something that neither Job nor his friends had discovered, namely, that the suffering of the righteous is not a token of God's enmity but of his love. It is not a punishment of their sins but a refinement of their

righteousness. It is not a preparation for destruction, but a protection from destruction.

The three friends [had] been wrong- suffering is not the proof of wickedness. And Job had been wrong- his suffering was not the proof of God's arbitrariness. Nor had God become his enemy. Elihu has come to put the argument on a new footing. (Henry, 2015)

Elihu was never introduced until just before he spoke. So, there are many unanswered questions, such as "When did he arrive?" "Who is he?" "Why is he there?" At the end of the book of Job, those questions remain unanswered. All we know is Elihu is the son of *"of Barakel the Buzite, of the family of Ram"* (v. 2), and he stayed silent during the entire debacle between Job and his three friends out of respect for his elders, as he is younger than any of the other four (v. 6).

However, from Elihu's retort, we learn, "He had two complaints. He was angry because Job justified himself rather than God, and he was angry at Job's three friends because they had found no answer, although they had declared Job to be in the wrong" (Piper, 1985).

For the three friends,

> the only way to explain Job's suffering was to say that God was punishing him for sin. Elihu shows that this is not the way to explain Job's suffering. The righteous do suffer. And their suffering is not a punishment for sin but a refinement of their righteousness. Suffering awakens their ear to new dimensions of God's reality and new depths of their own imperfection and need.

> Suffering deepens their faith and godliness. So the three friends of Job are wrong. (Piper, 1985)

For Job,

> He had no better explanation of his suffering than his three friends did. His conception of God's justice was basically the same as theirs. Only Job insisted he was righteous, and so he could not make his suffering fit with the justice of God. He became so exasperated at times that he thought of God as his enemy.
>
> God was NOT Job's enemy and Job is not as pure as he claims to be. God is in fact Job's loving Father. He has allowed this sickness to drag on for months because he loves Job, not because he hates him.
>
> The suffering has brought out the hidden sin of pride in Job. Now Job's ear has been opened to his remaining imperfection. Now he can repent and be cleansed and depend on God as he never had before. His suffering was not only an occasion for God to get glory over Satan (which we saw in chapters 1 and 2); it was also an occasion for God to deepen Job's insight and trust and godliness. (Piper, 1985)

So, even though there is much that is unclear about Elihu, his discourse brings clarity to a lot of what both sides of the debate had to say. In essence, he filled in the blanks and corrected misconceptions.

The Bottom Line

Chapter Twenty-Four
A Voice of Thunder

Chapter 38 The LORD Speaks

Then the LORD *spoke to Job out of the storm. He said:* [2] *"Who is this that obscures my plans with words without knowledge?* [3] *Brace yourself like a man; I will question you, and you shall answer me.* [4] *"Where were you when I laid the earth's foundation? Tell me, if you understand.* [5] *Who marked off its dimensions? Surely you know! Who stretched a measuring line across it?* [6] *On what were its footings set, or who laid its cornerstone—* [7] *while the morning stars sang together and all the angels shouted for joy?* [8] *"Who shut up the sea behind doors when it burst forth from the womb,* [9] *when I made the clouds its garment and wrapped it in thick darkness,* [10] *when I fixed limits for it and set its doors and bars in place,* [11] *when I said, 'This far you may come and no farther; here is where your proud waves halt'?* [12] *"Have you ever given orders to the morning, or shown the dawn its place,* [13] *that it might take the earth by the edges and shake the wicked out of it?* [14] *The earth takes shape like clay under a seal; its features stand out like those of a garment.* [15] *The wicked are denied their light, and their upraised arm is broken.* [16] *"Have you journeyed to the springs of the sea or walked in the recesses of the deep?* [17] *Have the gates of death been shown to you? Have you seen* the gates of the deepest darkness? ^{18} Have you comprehended the vast expanses of the earth? Tell me, if you know all this. ^{19} "What is the way to the abode of light? And where does darkness reside? ^{20} Can you take them to their places? Do you know the paths to their dwellings? ^{21} Surely you know, for you were already born! You have lived so many years! ^{22} "Have you entered the storehouses of the snow or seen the storehouses of the hail, ^{23} which I reserve for times of trouble, for days of war and battle? ^{24} What is the way to the place where the lightning is dispersed, or the place where the east winds are scattered over the earth? ^{25} Who cuts a channel for the torrents of rain, and a path for the thunderstorm, ^{26} to water a land where no one lives, an uninhabited desert, ^{27} to satisfy a desolate wasteland and make it sprout with grass? ^{28} Does the rain have a father? Who fathers the drops of dew? ^{29} From whose womb comes the ice? Who gives birth to the frost from the heavens ^{30} when the waters become hard as stone, when the surface of the deep is frozen? ^{31} "Can you bind the chains of the Pleiades? Can you loosen Orion's belt? ^{32} Can you bring forth the constellations in their seasons or lead out the Bear with its cubs? ^{33} Do you know the laws of the heavens? Can you set up God's dominion over the earth? ^{34} "Can you raise your voice to the clouds and cover yourself with a flood of water? ^{35} Do you send the lightning bolts on their way? Do they report to you, 'Here we are'? ^{36} Who gives the ibis wisdom or gives the rooster understanding? ^{37} Who has the wisdom to count the clouds? Who can tip over the water jars of the heavens ^{38} when the dust becomes hard and the clods of earth stick together? ^{39} "Do you hunt the prey for the lioness and satisfy the hunger of the lions ^{40} when they crouch in their dens or lie in wait in a thicket? ⁴¹ Who provides food for the raven when its young cry out to God and wander about for lack of food?

Chapter 39 The Lord Continues

"Do you know when the mountain goats give birth? Do you watch when the doe bears her fawn? ² Do you count the months till they bear? Do you know the time they give birth? ³ They crouch down and bring forth their young; their labor pains are ended. ⁴ Their young thrive and grow strong in the wilds; they leave and do not return.⁵ "Who let the wild donkey go free? Who untied its ropes? ⁶ I gave it the wasteland as its home, the salt flats as its habitat. ⁷ It laughs at the commotion in the town; it does not hear a driver's shout. ⁸ It ranges the hills for its pasture and searches for any green thing. ⁹ "Will the wild ox consent to serve you? Will it stay by your manger at night? ¹⁰ Can you hold it to the furrow with a harness? Will it till the valleys behind you? ¹¹ Will you rely on it for its great strength? Will you leave your heavy work to it? ¹² Can you trust it to haul in your grain and bring it to your threshing floor? ¹³ "The wings of the ostrich flap joyfully, though they cannot compare with the wings and feathers of the stork. ¹⁴ She lays her eggs on the ground and lets them warm in the sand, ¹⁵ unmindful that a foot may crush them, that some wild animal may trample them. ¹⁶ She treats her young harshly, as if they were not hers; she cares not that her labor was in vain, ¹⁷ for God did not endow her with wisdom or give her a share of good sense. ¹⁸ Yet when she spreads her feathers to run, she laughs at horse and rider. ¹⁹ "Do you give the horse its strength or clothe its neck with a flowing mane? ²⁰ Do you *make it leap like a locust, striking terror with its proud snorting? ^{21} It paws fiercely, rejoicing in its strength, and charges into the fray. ^{22} It laughs at fear, afraid of nothing; it does not shy away from the sword. ^{23} The quiver rattles against its side, along with the flashing spear and lance. ^{24} In frenzied excitement it eats up the ground; it cannot stand still when the trumpet sounds. ^{25} At the blast of the trumpet it snorts, 'Aha!' It catches the scent of battle from afar, the shout of commanders and the battle cry. ^{26} "Does the hawk take flight by your wisdom and spread its wings toward the south? ^{27} Does the eagle soar at your command and build its nest on high? ^{28} It dwells on a cliff and stays there at night; a rocky crag is its stronghold. ^{29} From there it looks for food; its eyes detect it from afar. ^{30} Its young ones feast on blood, and where the slain are, there it is."*

Chapter 40 The Lord Continues

The LORD said to Job: ^{2} "Will the one who contends with the Almighty correct him? Let him who accuses God answer him!" ^{3} Then Job answered the LORD: ^{4} "I am unworthy—how can I reply to you? I put my hand over my mouth. ^{5} I spoke once, but I have no answer— twice, but I will say no more." ^{6} Then the LORD spoke to Job out of the storm: ^{7} "Brace yourself like a man; I will question you, and you shall answer me. ^{8} "Would you discredit my justice? Would you condemn me to justify yourself? ^{9} Do you have an arm like God's, and can your voice thunder like his? ^{10} Then adorn yourself with glory and splendor, and clothe yourself in honor and majesty.^{11} Unleash the fury of your wrath, look at all who are proud and bring them low, ^{12} look at all who are proud and humble them, crush the wicked where they stand. ¹³ Bury them all in the dust together; shroud their faces in the grave. ¹⁴ Then I myself will admit to you that your own right hand can save you. ¹⁵ "Look at Behemoth, which I made along with you and which feeds on grass like an ox. ¹⁶ What strength it has in its loins, what power in the muscles of its belly! ¹⁷ Its tail sways like a cedar; the sinews of its thighs are close-knit. ¹⁸ Its bones are tubes of bronze, its limbs like rods of iron. ¹⁹ It ranks first among the works of God, yet its Maker can approach it with his sword. ²⁰ The hills bring it their produce, and all the wild animals play nearby. ²¹ Under the lotus plants it lies, hidden among the reeds in the marsh. ²² The lotuses conceal it in their shadow; the poplars by the stream surround it. ²³ A raging river does not alarm it; it is secure, though the Jordan should surge against its mouth. ²⁴ Can anyone capture it by the eyes, or trap it and pierce its nose?

Chapter 41 The Lord Continues

"Can you pull in Leviathan with a fishhook or tie down its tongue with a rope? ² Can you put a cord through its nose or pierce its jaw with a hook? ³ Will it keep begging you for mercy? Will it speak to you with gentle words? ⁴ Will it make an agreement with you for you to take it as your slave for life? ⁵ Can you make a pet of it like a bird or put it on a leash for the young women in your house? ⁶ Will traders barter for it? Will they divide it up among the merchants? ⁷ Can you fill its hide with harpoons or its head with fishing spears? ⁸ If you lay a hand on it, you will remember the struggle and never do it again! ⁹ Any hope of subduing it is false; the mere sight of it is overpowering. ¹⁰ No one is fierce enough to rouse it. Who then is able to stand against me? ¹¹ Who has a claim against me that I must pay? Everything under heaven belongs to me. ¹² "I will not fail to speak of Leviathan's limbs, its strength and its graceful form. ¹³ Who can strip off its outer coat? Who can penetrate its double coat of armor? ¹⁴ Who dares open the doors of its mouth, ringed about with fearsome teeth? ¹⁵ Its back has rows of shields tightly sealed together; ¹⁶ each is so close to the next that no air can pass between. ¹⁷ They are joined fast to one another; they cling together and cannot be parted. ¹⁸ Its snorting throws out flashes of light; its eyes are like the rays of dawn. ¹⁹ Flames stream from its mouth; sparks of fire shoot out. ²⁰ Smoke pours from its nostrils as from a boiling pot over burning reeds. ²¹ Its breath sets coals ablaze, and flames dart from its mouth. ²² Strength resides in its neck; dismay goes before it. ²³ The folds of its flesh are tightly joined; they are firm and immovable. ²⁴ Its chest is hard as rock, hard as a lower millstone. ²⁵ When it rises up, the mighty are terrified; they retreat before its thrashing. ²⁶ The sword that reaches it has no effect, nor does the spear or the dart or the javelin. ²⁷ Iron it treats like straw and bronze like rotten wood. ²⁸ Arrows do not make it flee; slingstones are like chaff to it. ²⁹ A club seems to it but a piece of straw; it laughs at the rattling of the lance. ³⁰ Its undersides are jagged potsherds, leaving a trail in the mud like a threshing sledge. ³¹ It makes the depths churn like a boiling caldron and stirs up the sea like a pot of ointment. ³² It leaves a glistening wake behind it; one would think the deep had white hair. ³³ Nothing on earth is its equal— a creature without fear. ³⁴ It looks down on all that are haughty; it is king over all that are proud."

God, who has been silent throughout this entire ordeal, suddenly appears on the scene amidst a whirlwind. From the whirlwind, God speaks. Apparently displeased with Job, God asks who obscures His plans with empty words that do not bestow knowledge. He instructs Job to brace himself as a man because He has some questions for him and He expects answers.

He asks Job where he was when God laid the earth's foundation (v. 4a), who shut up the seas behind doors (v. 8), if he had ever given orders to the morning (v. 12), if he ever journeyed to the springs of the sea or walked the recesses of the deep (v. 16), if the gates of hell had been shown to him (v. 17), if he had entered the storehouse of the snow (v. 22), if the rain has a father (v. 28), if he can bring forth the constellations in their seasons (v. 32), if he knows when the mountain goats give birth (Ch. 39, v. 1), who let the wild donkeys go free (v. 5), if he gave the horse its strength (v. 19), if the hawk flies at his wisdom (v. 26), and much, much more.

In the midst of asking these questions, God says, *"Tell me, if you understand,"* (v. 4b) and *"Tell me, if you know all this,"* (v. 18b) and *"Surely you know, for you were already born! You have lived so many years!"* (v. 21).

In several of the previous chapters, Job had spoken with such boldness and certainty as to profess his wisdom about God's ways. So, God demonstrates to Job how little he actually does know about how and why God operates.

In Chapter 40, God asks, *"Will the one who contends with the Almighty correct him?"* (v. 2a). Then, He demands his accuser answer Him. Without hesitation, Job confesses he is unworthy to answer God. He admits he spoke once, but he has no answer for God, so he will speak no more. God continues to speak from the whirlwind and once again tells Job to brace himself and be a man, for God would question him and Job would answer (v. 7).

God asks Job is he would discredit His justice and condemn God to justify himself (v. 8). He asks if Job has an arm like God's and if he does; then, unleash the fury of his wrath and bring the proud low and humble them (v. 11-12). God told Job if he could do that then He would admit to Job that he could save himself. But, of course, Job could not admit that because he holds no such power.

In Chapter 41, God asks Job, *"Can you pull in Leviathan with a fishhook or tie down its tongue with a rope?"* (v. 1). The rest of the chapter discusses the uniqueness of Leviathan and its strength. The chapter closes with these words: *"Nothing on earth is its equal— a creature without fear. It looks down on all that are haughty; it is king over all that are proud"* (v. 33-34).

The characteristics Leviathan possesses is synonymous with the characteristics God possesses. God is the King over all, and He will humble the proud. He can make them bend or break before Him (Isaiah 2:11).

Chapter Twenty-Five
A Heartfelt Apology

Chapter 42 Job Replies to God
Then Job replied to the L*ORD*: *² "I know that you can do all things; no purpose of yours can be thwarted. ³ You asked, 'Who is this that obscures my plans without knowledge?' Surely I spoke of things I did not understand, things too wonderful for me to know. ⁴ "You said, 'Listen now, and I will speak; I will question you, and you shall answer me.' ⁵ My ears had heard of you but now my eyes have seen you. ⁶ Therefore I despise myself and repent in dust and ashes."*

Job gives a heartfelt, humble reply to God. He admits he knows the power of God, who can do all things. In answering God's question about who obscures God's plans without knowledge and wisdom, Job admits he spoke about things he does not understand. He admits the inner workings of God's creations are too wonderful for him to comprehend. Job recalls God telling him to listen while He spoke because He wanted an answer when He was done. Job says his ears heard God, and his eyes had seen Him. As a result, Job says, *"Therefore I despise myself and repent in dust and ashes"* (v. 6).

Job learned a great lesson when he sat quietly and listened to God. God is omniscient. When we enter into prayer and have open discourse with God, we would be wise to listen to God to receive instruction from Him. God has our best interest at heart, and He wants us to do well in all we do.

Chapter Twenty-Six
Abundant Blessings

Epilogue

⁷ After the L<small>ORD</small> *had said these things to Job, he said to Eliphaz the Temanite, "I am angry with you and your two friends, because you have not spoken the truth about me, as my servant Job has. ⁸ So now take seven bulls and seven rams and go to my servant Job and sacrifice a burnt offering for yourselves. My servant Job will pray for you, and I will accept his prayer and not deal with you according to your folly. You have not spoken the truth about me, as my servant Job has." ⁹ So Eliphaz the Temanite, Bildad the Shuhite and Zophar the Naamathite did what the* L<small>ORD</small> *told them; and the* L<small>ORD</small> *accepted Job's prayer. ¹⁰ After Job had prayed for his friends, the* L<small>ORD</small> *restored his fortunes and gave him twice as much as he had before. ¹¹ All his brothers and sisters and everyone who had known him before came and ate with him in his house. They comforted and consoled him over all the trouble the* L<small>ORD</small> *had brought on him, and each one gave him a piece of silver and a gold ring. ¹² The* L<small>ORD</small> *blessed the latter part of Job's life more than the former part. He had fourteen thousand sheep, six thousand camels, a thousand yoke of oxen and a thousand donkeys. ¹³ And he also had seven sons and three daughters. ¹⁴ The first daughter he named Jemimah, the second Keziah and the third*

The Bottom Line

Keren-Happuch. ⁱ⁵ Nowhere in all the land were there found women as beautiful as Job's daughters, and their father granted them an inheritance along with their brothers. ¹⁶ After this, Job lived a hundred and forty years; he saw his children and their children to the fourth generation. ¹⁷ And so Job died, an old man and full of years.

After God and Job spoke with one another, God turned his attention to Eliphaz, the first of Job's friends to speak during Job's ordeal. God tells Eliphaz he and the others did not speak truthfully about Him as Job had. He tells them to *"take seven bulls and seven rams and go to my servant Job and sacrifice a burnt offering for yourselves"* (v. 8a). God continued by telling them, his servant Job would pray for them, and He would accept Job's prayer for them. God said he refused to deal with their folly.

The three friends obeyed God and did as He directed. After Job was obedient and prayed for his friends, God *"restored his fortunes and gave him twice as much as he had before"* (10b). His family and friends came and fellowshipped with him, bringing him gifts. Job was blessed in his latter years even more so than in his former years. He lived to be 140 years of age and was blessed to see his children and their children of four generations.

When God spoke, Job instantly stopped complaining. He humbled himself under the mighty hand of God. He opened his ears to hear "what thus saith the Lord." In doing so, he was able to take his eyes off his situation and see to someone else's needs. In this case, the 'someone' happened to be three people:

Eliphaz, Bildad, and Zophar. His friends needed God's forgiveness for their folly, wagging tongues, and positions of superiority. They had actually talked down to God's man servant, ridiculed him, and falsely accused him. For this, they needed to repent and ask forgiveness.

The Bottom Line

Chapter Twenty-Seven
Final Thoughts

Now that we have examined the complete Book of Job, we can now discuss **the bottom line** in a little more detail. As I stated earlier, in each and every situation we face in our lives, there is a bottom line. Viewing Job's catastrophe of the loss of his family, cattle, wealth, and servants and the physical attack on his body, and the harsh rebuke of his friends, along with his harsh words towards God, stemming from a spirit of pride, there is much we can say.

However, we must examine the entire scenario and not simply one component or another. Remember, Job was doing extremely well until Satan decided he would be an excellent candidate for attack. Satan was walking to and fro across the earth seeking whom he could devour, someone who would turn his back on God. He was sure Job would be an excellent candidate. He was certain Job only praised God because God had blessed him abundantly. Upon receiving God's permission, Satan set to work.

Prior to Satan's attack, Job was not only concerned with himself, but he was concerned with the lives and well-being of others. He counseled others and prayed for others. For all intents and purposes, we cannot label Job as a self-centered person.

However, when Job was afflicted, his attention turned inward. He wanted to know why he was chosen to be a target of God. He wanted to know what could have been so bad that God had chosen to afflict him in the worst possible ways a human could be afflicted. The severity of his turmoil led him to complain and utter harsh words to the god he loved and respected.

When we are faced with trials, what may be buried deep within us will rise to the surface. Job, a man who loved God, also had the spirit of pride. Although he didn't take credit for his riches and his blessings, which he knew came from God, he found no fault with himself.

Was this the reason God permitted Satan to have his way with Job? It may be part of it, but I believe God wanted to show Satan he is not as powerful as he thinks. **But mainly**, God wants us to take our focus off ourselves and our situation and live for others. He wants us to love others as ourselves. Matthew 22:39 says, *"And the second is like it: 'Love your neighbor as yourself.'"* He wants us to be selfless, like He is. John 3:16 says, *"For God so loved the world that he gave his one and only Son, that whoever believes in him shall not perish but have eternal life."*

God loves us so much that He gave His only son to come to this world of sin to die on a cross, so we could be re-united/reconciled with Him. He loves us so much that He did not want to see us perish and succumb to sin. With the death of His son Jesus, we were provided a way back to the Father.

Like Job, we can find our way back to the Father and into His good graces when we step outside of ourselves and attend to the needs of others. Job had a serious issue of pride, but when God spoke, which is all Job wanted, Job listened. He humbled himself, and he prayed for his friends who desperately needed God's forgiveness.

Can you take your eyes off your own situation and give your attention to others? When Job took his eyes off the devastation he was enduring and the suffering he had been afflicted with, before he knew it, his trials had come to an end.

What are you faced with today that you want God's hand to move upon? Are you sitting and stewing in your situation while being unable to change it?

If that is the bottom line of your situation, turn your attention to someone or something else. Be productive, as time is passing you by. Don't waste another day focusing and complaining about a situation you cannot change. Allow God to be God for you. He is the one who is omniscient, omnipresent, and omnipotent. He is in full control. Move out of His way and watch your situation turn around.

That, my friends, is the bottom line!

The Bottom Line

References

"Bildad." (2014). *The Encyclopedia Britannica*. The Editors of Encyclopedia Britannica. britannica.com. December 25, 2014.

Bury, G. W. *The Land of Uz*. (1911 (original), 1998 reprint).

Christian Truth Center. (2015). *Three Main Levels of Faith.* http://www.christiantruthcenter.com/the-three-main-levels-of-faith

"Covert." Oxford Dictionary Online. Dec. 2014.

"Eliphaz the Temanite." (2014). *The Encyclopedia Britannica*. The Editors of Encyclopedia Britannica. britannica.com. December 25, 2014.

Gill, J. (2004-2014). *Gill's Exposition of the Entire Bible*. Biblehub.com. December 25, 2014.

Hahn, R. (2012). *Book of Job*. Roger Hahn and the Christian Resource Institute. crivoice.org. December 24, 2014

Henry, M. *Matthew Henry's Concise Commentary*. Via biblehub.com December 25, 2014.

Miller. B. (2013). *Let Your Petitions Be Made Known To God: What is Intercessory Prayer* Christ Unlimited Ministries – http://BibleResources.org

O'Neal, S. (2014). *Why People in the Bible Tore Their Clothes.* aboutreligion.com December 24, 2014.

"Overt." Oxford Dictionary Online. Dec. 2014.

Piper, J. July 21, 1985 "Job: Rebuked in Suffering." *Old Testament Biblical Figures.*

Gift of Salvation
for Non-Believers

"For all have sinned, and come short of the glory of God."
Romans 3:23

This section was written especially for non-believers, those who have not accepted the gift of salvation. The gift of salvation saves souls from eternal dam-nation and is a free gift offered by God himself.

John 3:16-18 says, *"For God so loved the world, that he gave his only begotten Son, that whosoever believeth in him should not perish, but have everlasting life. For God sent not his Son into the world to condemn the world; but that the world through him might be saved. He that believeth on him is not condemned: but he that believeth not is condemned already, because he hath not believed in the name of the only begotten Son of God."*

This section of scripture tells us God's purpose for giving His son Jesus to the world. The world was in a bad condition. The world was overwrought with sin; the people were living for fleshly desires rather than for God's desires.

As a result of the world's conditions, God decided that He would offer the perfect sacrifice that would save the world from being a place where people were lost and had no hope. He decided that His own son could stand in proxy for the sin-filled world, taking all sin upon Himself.

So Jesus came, born of a virgin, to save this dying world. He walked on this earth for 33 ½ years, doing the work of His Heavenly Father. At the appointed time, He died by way of crucifixion upon a cross at Calvary, on Golgatha's hill. He shed his blood and died for you and for me. Because His blood was pure, it paid the penalty for all unrighteousness and gave those who believe in Him direct access to His father's throne.

Scripture tells us in Matthew 27:51 that the veil of the temple was ripped in two from top to bottom, at the moment that Jesus' spirit left His body. As a result of the veil's removal, we are no longer required to have a high priest make intercession for us. We, as the children of the Most High God, are able to approach the throne God for ourselves, and Jesus sits on the right hand of the Father making intercession for us.

But what is even more miraculous than God offering His own son as the perfect sacrifice was the fact that when Jesus was placed in grave clothes and placed in a tomb, He only remained there until the third day. God would not have it that His son would remain in the heart of the earth forever. In order for people to believe in the awesome power of God and His dear son Jesus, a miracle had to be performed. So, on the third day, after Jesus died on the cross, He was resurrected, demonstrating the omnipotence of God. This very act was the act that would cause people to believe in a god that reigns supreme and holds the power of the universe in His very hands, a god that could save them from themselves.

Today, if you are an unbeliever, you can change your destiny. You can change where you will spend your eternity. Our Heavenly Father gives us the freedom of choice about how we want to live our life here on earth and how we want to spend eternity. In Deuteronomy 30:19, God boldly declares, *"I call heaven and earth to record this day against you, that I have set before you life and death, blessing and cursing: therefore choose life, that both thou and thy seed may live."*

So, dear friend what choice will you make today? Will you spend your eternity with the Creator or will you suffer Hell's eternal flames? Again, the choice is yours. Just as the men aboard the ship who were with Jonah became believers, you too can make a choice to accept the only one and true living God as your god.

If after reading the above passages, you have decided that you want to spend your eternity in Heaven with God, the creator, and His son Jesus, and the Holy Spirit, read through what has affectionately come to be known as the Roman's Road. This is the road to salvation. As you read through the scriptures that comprise the Roman's Road, you will also read the explanation for each scripture so you will have clarity about what you are reading and confessing.

The Roman's Road to Salvation

The road to salvation begins with Romans 3:23 which declares, *"For all have sinned, and come short of the glory of God."* This scripture explains that everyone has come short of God's glory and needs redemption. Then Romans 6:23a states, *"For the wages of sin is death."* Here, we learn that the consequence of living a life of sin is death. Everyone will experience physical death as a result of the sin committed in the garden of Eden, but those who commit themselves to a life of sin will suffer eternal damnation in the lake of fire (Rev. 19).

Continue with the rest of verse 6:23 that says, *"but the gift of God is eternal life through Jesus Christ our Lord."* There is an alternative to suffering eternal damnation. We can accept the gift of salvation by accepting Jesus as our personal lord and savior. Then, Romans 5:8 says, *"But God commendeth his love toward us, in that, while we were yet sinners, Christ died for us."* We are able to receive the gift of salvation because Christ came to earth and shed His blood for us on the cross.

Continue to Romans 10: 9-10 which says, *"That if thou shalt confess with thy mouth the Lord Jesus, and shalt believe in thine heart that God hath raised him from the dead, thou shalt be saved. For with the heart man believeth unto righteousness; and with the mouth confession is made unto salvation."* If we confess with our mouths that Jesus is the son of God, that he came and died for our sins, and that God raised Him from the dead, we will receive salvation.

Finish with Romans 10:13, which states, *"For whosoever shall call upon the name of the Lord shall be saved."* Call upon the name of God by saying these words, **"Lord Jesus, come into my heart and save me Lord. I believe that you are the Son of God who came and died on the cross for my sins. I believe that you rose from the grave. I also believe that you now sit in heaven on the right side of the Father, making intersession for me. I accept you as my Lord and my Savior."**

Now that you have confessed with your mouth that Jesus is the son of God and that He died for our sins and rose from the grave, **YOU ARE NOW SAVED!!!!** You will spend your eternity in heaven.

The next step is very important- you must find a bible-based church that teaches the word of God and confesses the Lord Jesus Christ to be the son of God. Don't delay. Do this immediately. Do not leave yourself open to the enemy. Get connected with the saints of the Most High God and keep yourself covered with the unspotted blood of the lamb.

Here is my prayer for you.

Father God,

I thank you for the opportunity to minister your word to the unsaved, the unchurched, and the uncommitted. Father God, I pray now for the souls who have just received the gift of salvation. Lord Father, they have opened their hearts to you, and I know that you have received them into your kingdom and written their names in the Book of Life. Father God, I pray that you will touch their lives and show yourself mightily before them. Let their eyes be opened by the scales falling off, allowing them to see clearly.

Father God, I even pray for the backslider, those who have turned away from you after receiving the gift of salvation. You said in your word that you desire that none would perish. So Lord, I send your word to them right now praying that they would confess the iniquity in their heart, repent, and turn from their evil ways, so that they may receive a life of abundance. You said in your word in Matthew Chapter 14, that every knee shall bow before you and every tongue will confess that Jesus is Lord.

Father God, I pray now that we all come under subjection to your word and that we will humbly submit our lives to

you. I ask all these things in the name of my Lord and Savior Jesus Christ.
Amen, Amen, Amen!!!!

I will continue to pray for your success in your walk with God. Remember, this spiritual walk that you are about to embark on will not be an easy walk, but remember, the race is not given to the swift but to those who endure to the end.

Be blessed with heaven's best. I love you!

ABOUT THE AUTHOR

Dr. Cassundra White-Elliott resides in California with her family, where as an English/Education professor she teaches at various community colleges and universities.

When writing, she writes with the direction of the Holy Spirit, in an effort to share with God's people all that He has for them.

In addition to teaching and writing, Dr. White-Elliott also serves as an evangelistic teacher. She is also the founder of International Women's Commission, a ministry that serves the needs of the entire person, by attending to healing the mind, body, soul, and spirit.

Dr. White-Elliott holds a Ph.D. in Education, a Master's in English Composition, and a Bachelor's in Education.

Dr. White-Elliott is also the founder of CLF Publishing, LLC.

For your publishing needs, go online to www.clfpublishing.org.

The Bottom Line

OTHER BOOKS BY THE AUTHOR

(All books can be purchased at www.creativemindsbookstore or amazon.com)

The Bottom Line

From Despair, through Determination, to Victory!

A lot can happen during a span of 40 years. The life of Dr. Cassundra White-Elliott has been anything but uneventful. From a fun-loving childhood sprinkled with incidents of abuse to a tumultuous young adulthood to a stable, secure adult life, she has experienced a full life, with much more to come. Her story is inspiring and motivating.

If anyone lacks hope, reading Dr. White-Elliott's autobiography will propel him/her into an attitude of "Maybe I can." This attitude, if nurtured and developed, will grow into an attitude of "Yes, I can." Throughout her life, Cassundra has always held in her heart the belief that she could achieve anything that she had a made-up mind to embark upon. She was determined to achieve her heart's desires, doing what God has called her to do. She takes no credit for herself. All the glory goes to God, for He is her driving force. In Him, she lives, moves, and has her being.

Through the Storm

Through the Storm was duly inspired by the avaricious cloud of depression that decided to hover overhead of my daily existence in the latter part of 2007. Although I found it extremely difficult, I was once again compelled to not be defeated by just another snare that the enemy, the trickster, set for me. Once again, or more appropriately I should say *continuously*, he has exerted pernicious efforts to snatch the very life out of me by causing me to wallow in despair and to believe that I had been overcome by failure when in actuality and all reality, I was just experiencing a temporary setback. During those cloudy days, I had to remind myself daily that even though I was a target of the enemy, I am and will always be a child of the Most High god, Jehovah, who is my rock, my stability.

Unleashed Anger, Anger Unleashed

Introduction
What Is This Book All About?

As I prepared to embark upon the adventure of writing this book, I had to prepare myself to also be transparent. I have found that being transparent is required in order for healing to transpire, healing for all those that peruse the pages of this book and myself. And I may as well tell you that today, at the onset of this project, I have not been totally delivered from my condition of being an anger-filled person. However, I am definitely a work in progress. I have made strides with the assistance of my Lord and Savior, Jesus Christ, who is the head of my life. Without his love, guidance, and teachings, I would not be the woman of God I am today. I shudder to think where I could be instead and will therefore not entertain the thought.

Public Speaking in the Spiritual Arena

Gain the tools to speak successfully in public, with particular focus on the spiritual arena.

Where is Your Joppa?

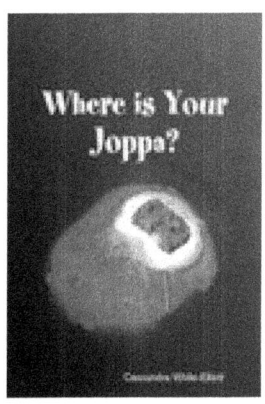

Where is Your Joppa? was written for the express purpose of illustrating God's call for obedience in the lives of believers with respect to the individual call that He has on each of our lives. As you read throughout the various chapters, notice that the emphasis is placed on our persistent disobedience in answering God's call in a specific area of our lives. We have become a people who are similar to the Israelites when they found themselves in the middle of the wilderness, following their exodus from Egypt. Before God, they murmured and complained about their current life conditions and failed to be obedient to God's statutes delivered through His servant Moses. Their persistent disobedience caused them to lose the opportunity to see and enter the Promised Land. I ask you, "What has your disobedience cost you?" "Was your disobedience worth what it cost you?"

Mayhem in the Hamptons

Romero and Yolanda optimistically plan for the day that is going to change their lives from being single persons to a couple who is united in holy matrimony. They, along with their parents, close friends and family, fly over to the infamous Hamptons, where only the rich and famous vacation, to have their dream wedding at the five-star Hampton Suites located on a peninsula in the Hamptons. Little do they know that their perfect day will turn out to be less than perfect when their wedding planner Mariesha Coleman suddenly goes missing!

Mayhem in the Hamptons is a tale that shares how the horrors of a woman's past can come back to haunt her in more than one way and the impact it can have on anyone who gets in the way.

The Preacher's Daughter

Tinisha, the daughter of a preacher, is a twenty-six year old God-fearing young woman endeavoring to complete law school so that she can make her mark in the courtroom. Working in one of the late-night clubs in Hollywood to earn money to pay her own way through school, Tinisha soon learns that life doesn't always go as planned. Finding her strength in her faith, Tinisha constantly finds herself praying as she watches God move miraculously in her life.

Preacher's Son

Romero Turner is a private investigator with a promising future. As he continues to build his career, he is excited about the cases he undertakes. However, his father Pastor Theodore Turner has other plans for his son's life. In the midst of trying to save his client's husband from Sylvester Domingo, a ruthless crime lord, Romero must try to salvage his relationship with his father. He must decide if ministry or life as a detective is in his future.

Lord, Teach Me to be a Blessing!

Lord, Teach Me to be a Blessing! will change a person's mentality from being centered around "me, myself, and I" to focusing on "others." The world system teaches us that it is acceptable to place ourselves above others in an attempt to get ahead and even to survive. Herbert Spencer coined the phrase *'survival of the fittest'* after reading Charles Darwin's theory of evolution. This concept of surpassing and outdoing others is the world's philosophy. However, the word of God does not subscribe to or promote this self-centered ideology, and therefore, neither should believers. We must hold fast to the truths outlined in Holy Scripture: *"Love thy neighbor as you love thyself"* (James 2:8) and *"It is more blessed to give than to receive"* (Acts 20:35).

While holding God's truths to be self-evident, we must demonstrate them to others, thereby showing them the way of the Lord of how to be a blessing to someone *rather* than looking to receive a blessing.

After the Dust Settles

Throughout the journey of life, we all experience ups and downs and joys and pains. Most of us successfully find solutions to the situations/problems we encounter, but we often avoid dealing with the attached emotions. If we continue to ignore the emotions of pain, hurt, disappointment, anger, etc., we set ourselves up for destruction. Our families, our cultures, and our society tell us to be strong, to keep our chin up, and to grin and bear it. However, these methods of avoidance can lead us to strokes due to the undue amount of pressure we place on ourselves and/or mental illness from being unable to cope with the emotional baggage we have accumulated.

In ***After the Dust Settles***, Dr. C. White-Elliott shares several situations that we all may encounter at one time or another in our lifetime and how to successfully navigate through them, so we can find ourselves emotionally healthy after the dust has settled and the situation has been rectified.

A Diamond in the Rough

A Diamond in the Rough Architecture Firm was built and is owned and operated by lead architect Kyra Fraser. For the last five years, Kyra has been extremely successful in business, but her love life leaves much to be desired.

Kyra has set high standards for herself and does not wish to take a man in any condition and attempt to make him over. She is looking for someone who is drama free, well educated, very cultured, fun-loving, good looking, self-motivated, and the list goes on.

Will Kyra find the man of her dreams, or will her dream just continue to be a dream?

As you delve into this page-turning novel, Kyra's reality will unfold as you are drawn into her world of design, love and office drama- which includes her best friend's husband who is looking for love in all the wrong places.

365 Days of Encouragement

Just as our brain requires oxygen obtained from the air we breathe to sustain our mortal bodies, our spirit requires revitalization and encouragement in order to be strengthened each and every day of our lives. The revitalization and encouragement needed for the spirit of man comes directly from the word of God and assists us in walking according to the way of our heavenly Father. ***365 Days of Encouragement*** provides a scripture a day for each day of the year. Along with the daily scripture is a brief note of commentary also for the benefit of edifying the saints of God. It is my prayer that the people of God would live a fulfilled life through Christ Jesus. Knowing His word and understanding we can walk in the fulfillment thereof is empowering. We are instructed in II Timothy 2:15, "Study to shew thyself approved unto God, a workman that needeth not to be ashamed, rightly dividing the word of truth" (KJV).

A Mother's Heart

    A Mother's Heart shares the unconditional love of mothers through a compilation of testimonies. Each testimony serves as a tribute to a special mother. The children of the represented mothers have lovingly written about their childhood, young adult life and/or older adult experiences they shared with their mother. As you read the writers' reflections, you will feel the expressions of love exude from the pages.

The purpose of this book is two-fold. First, it honors those mothers who stood by their children through the trials of life and showered them with unconditional love. Second, the book is a source of encouragement for mothers who may feel inadequate and question whether or not they are actually suited for motherhood.

Mothers may not be perfect, but they are definitely unmatched by any other category of person on God's green earth!

Power of a Woman

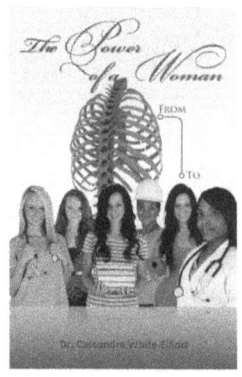

The ongoing conversation about the value of a woman is presented from a different perspective in **The Power of a Woman**. Dr. Cassundra White-Elliott presents a biblical perspective of women and compares it to the worldview of both yesterday and today. This comparison seeks to illustrate God's intended purpose for His uniquely designed creation: *woman*. Dr. Elliott shares God's truth about pre-imposed limitations set by man versus the limitations God Himself set for woman in addition to the wealth of liberality He gave her.
Women's creativity and abilities are not meant to be stifled. They are meant to be utilized to bring glory to God, to help sustain and nurture their families, and to move the world forward. Knowing God's truth will show women how to celebrate and appreciate who they are as well as one another!

Women, let's take the blinders off, lift our heads up, and march forward, side by side with men, and bring glory and honor to God! Take your rightful place with a gentle smile and grace and be who God called you to be!

A Touch in the Dark

Dr. Teri Langston is enjoying life with her husband Reggie and doing all that she loves to do: traveling, eating good food, spending time with family and friends, and re-decorating her home. Her career is doing well, and life is grand. In her world, there is nothing else that she needs- except a little healing. From the recesses of her mind, her past sneaks back in to haunt her and remind her of traumatic events she once endured. In the midst of living fantasies fulfilled, Teri finds herself grasping for peace in the middle of a still, quiet storm. Surrounded by her loving family, Teri wonders if the memories will ever fade, if the uncomfortable feelings will ever subside, and if she will ever turn the past loose. Take this journey with Teri as she laughs, cries, rejoices, and looks for answers. Will she find the peace she longs for or will her suffering be prolonged?

Broken Chains

Broken Chains is an in-depth survey of five life-changing tragedies that can and will serve as chains to bind us if we are not watchful and mindful of their potential effects. In our lifetimes, we may all experience death of loved ones, sexual abuse, broken relationships, promiscuity, and sickness and disease. These everyday life occurrences can have detrimental effects on the remaining years of our lives and change our existence, unless we deal with them in a healthy manner.

Broken Chains not only brings to light the detrimental effects of five life-changing tragedies, but it also shares how anyone who experiences them can be healed and delivered from their effects.

If you have experienced death of a loved one, sexual abuse, a broken relationship, the effects of promiscuity, and/or sickness and disease and have not been able to rid yourself of the emotions attached to them or specific resulting behaviors, ***Broken Chains*** is for you. God designed each of us for a purpose, and He has an intended end for us to achieve. In order for us to effectively achieve our God-given purpose, we must be free of chains that bind us. It is not God's desire that we become immobilized by life's events. His desire is for us to be healed, delivered and set free. Be healed today, in the name of the Lord Jesus Christ!

I Have Fallen

Do you know anyone who has committed his/her life to Christ but has done something unseemly that you would never expect a Christian to do? How did you feel about that person or what the person did? Did you pass judgment? What if that person were you? How would you feel if you made a misstep and no one forgave you and instead began to treat you differently? How do you feel when you are judged for past mistakes or lifestyles that are no longer part of your life?

This book shares four true stories of Christians who have made missteps during their walk with God. The purpose is not to air their dirty laundry, but to demonstrate our humanness and our vulnerability. None of us are exempt from making errors and falling into sin. It can happen to any of us.

The solution for these dilemmas is for the person who fell into sin to make a life-changing move and turn away from the sin, repent and ask God for forgiveness. His arms are waiting!

The next solution is for those who witness the sin or know of it. Pray and be of comfort to the one who has fallen. Lead him/her back to the path of righteousness. Love thy neighbor and treat him/her as you want to be treated!

Fear Not

Fear affects people on a daily basis. It can prevent them from opening up and sharing their most heartfelt emotions, trying a new activity, achieving their dream, meeting new people, attaining desired accomplishments, going back to school, etc.
2 Timothy 1:7 declares, *"For God hath not given us the spirit of fear; but of power, and of love, and of a sound mind."*

www.ingramcontent.com/pod-product-compliance
Lightning Source LLC
Chambersburg PA
CBHW070801100426
42742CB00012B/2215